Global Family Office Investing

Chad Hagan

Global Family Office Investing

Exploring the Practices of Single- and Multi-Family Offices

palgrave
macmillan

Chad Hagan
Hagan Capital
Roswell, GA, USA

ISBN 978-3-030-18223-6 ISBN 978-3-030-18224-3 (eBook)
https://doi.org/10.1007/978-3-030-18224-3

This Palgrave Macmillan imprint is published by the registered company Springer Nature Switzerland AG
The registered company address is: Gewerbestrasse 11, 6330 Cham, Switzerland

Preface

This book is for financial professionals, financial industry executives, and professionals in management. The goal in this publication is to provide useful intelligence into the global practice of single family offices (SFOs) and multifamily offices (MFOs) and to provide insight into the commonalties SFOs and MFOs have with the global economy. A more direct intention of this publication is to give professionals insight into the dynamics of the family offices; commons family office structures, and concise history of family offices.

One hundred years ago a wealthy individual would have their team draft trusts and foundation by-laws and order them to fund the accounts; only an industry titan or industry thought leader would have had the vison to construct a single office in America to administer to descendants. While some did form family offices, the bulk of modern family offices owe their existence to the private European banking model, which grouped together family money in partnerships, unregulated and unincorporated with general partners and limited partners. Provisions were made for daughters, often as a dowry or by offering the male spouse a partnership in the family venture, and banking families often intermarried.

I trace the modern family office structure as we know it to Europe. In the middle ages, private finance and trading houses established territories and financed royal families, aristocrats, ecclesiastical princes, and state operations. In the sixteenth and seventeenth centuries, many of these families became very powerful and developed into international investment concerns. Families branched out to other European capitals and some moved to the Middle East and Far East. In time these financial families immigrated to the US and developed private banking companies which were capitalized by family money. Some groups formed licensed banking companies to manage commercial investment concerns and in return helped bolster America's burgeoning financial system. One of the best known examples is the Warburg family in America. Descendant Paul Warburg, a German-born American, established the core architecture of the Federal Reserve and was rumored to be the inspiration for the fictional character "Daddy Warbucks," while his nephew Eric M. Warburg established the private equity firm Warburg Pincus. The Warburg's are a marquee example, but there exist many other prominent financial families responsible for developing the family office structure. Families like the Angelli's, Kennedy's, Rockefeller's, and the Paul Allen family have all pushed the idea of what a family office and family shareholder group should be, how it should progress, and why it should exist.

As this book covers the globe, I have remained conscious of the political differences that can arise in documenting details of global wealth; the reader will find that my center of reference is market-based capitalism, and my world view of economics, industry, and civilization is based on Western civilization. I have traveled these paths and witnessed these developments. As a long-term investor, family office founder, and economic analyst, I have spent the better part of fifteen years working side-by-side with some of the world's wealthiest family offices—including aristocratic households and corporate heirs from tercentenary commercial concerns—not to mention talented financier's and countless small family offices.

Data and Terminology

The acronyms: SFO, MFO, FO all stand for family offices of some sort. At times, in the industry, family offices are styled as: FOS. Regardless, in this publication SFO means single family office: MFO means multifamily/multifamily office, and FO means family office.

All of the GDP measurements in this book represent GDP at purchaser's prices and are also listed in GDP per capita. I have used GDP per capita to measure standards of living and development, which more than often lead to wealth in democracies and market-based economies. I have also elected to use past emissions data to show a snapshot of industrial development.

In this publication, I have included information relevant to family offices (both single and multifamily office) in democracy and republic governments with liberal trade policies and free markets as judged by groups such as the World Bank, the Economist Intelligence Unit, and other monitors mentioned below.

All data used was compiled from the following institutions:

- The Maddison Historical Statistics Project, University of Groningen. The project measures, Real GDP per capita in 2011 USD, and population.
- Federal Reserve, Survey of Consumer Finances (2016 Survey).
- National Bureau of Economic Research (NBER), Cambridge, Massachusetts.
- OECD, Organization for Economic Co-operation and Development.
- The Bureau of Labor Statistics, United States Department of Labor.
- World Bank Group, Washington, D.C.

Data outcomes were averaged, with defined numbers being used if there was sufficient support.

Roswell, GA, USA
February 2021

Chad Hagan

Acknowledgments

This book is based on research and firsthand experience conducted for nearly twenty years. I am forever grateful to a number of institutions for assistance, both scholarly and with this publication: Harvard University, the London School of Economics, the British Library of Political and Economic Science (LSE Library), the British Library, the National Archives (England), the National Archives (United States), the Library of Congress, and the Maddison Historical Statistics Project at the University of Groningen.

I would like to thank Tula Weiss, my editor at Palgrave Macmillan, and the staff and executives at Palgrave Macmillan and Springer Nature for supporting this publication.

I thank my manuscript editor Scotty Brewington. I am very grateful for her talented support.

Finally, I thank my Atlanta group of readers: Jim Eppelin, Scotty Brewington, Matthew Divenere, Bill Trainor, and Phil Curtis.

Acknowledgments

Author Disclosure

In writing this book I realized I needed to list a few explanations of how I know certain information and how I came about to writing it.

To begin, it is important to note that I am not sharing any confidential information. Most information in this publication is public. Additionally, the majority of this intelligence information has been gathered in private practice and then correlated with research to test validity.

To go into more detail, I founded a single family office and I am a researcher who has spent close to twenty years working in my field. Apart from having natural access to this world of family offices, I have had a personal mandate to develop and refine the structure that is a family office.

As you will discover in this publication, I find family offices to be a brilliant wealth management, estate planning and succession vehicle. They are also exceptional expert networks, opportunity sources for family office members and employees and a convenient funding source for family-funded charitable passions from philanthropy to businesses endeavors. I also feel very strongly that a family office is one of the most effective ways to conserve generational, family-oriented asset and to ownership transfer in common law countries.

Contents

List of Figures

1

Introduction

The concept of a single family office, family office, or private office generally denotes a hybrid entity of best practice that continues to reinvent itself, much like competitive marketplace firms. The main difference is fiduciary as family offices tend to be private and oriented toward preservation, even if that means a more concise record keeping of the spending of one's fortune. One of the main components of a successful family office is the central value of administration and observation. The media and press paint a colorful picture of family offices (FO) as a billionaire's private office, hardwired to generate obscene profits and take on unregulated risks for the sole benefit of increasing the fortune. They also suggest family offices are merely management hubs to combine the oversight of trust funds and private jet bookings, and that the management office is managed by prototypical ivy leaguers, Oxbridge males, or a set of grand écoles educated analysts in Geneva, playing with billions beneath rotating priceless art. While this has some truth to it, family offices are no longer just for royal households, plutocrats or billionaires. There are many more comfortably rich and moderately wealthy families' in the world than there are billionaires.[1]

Throughout this book I discuss family businesses and that is for a few reasons—a successful family business is the most organic way to start a family office. It is a natural progression to see a family business transform into a family office; over time the family business may no longer suit the family

[1]The World's Billionaires (2018), Forbes calculated 2,208 people who were billionaires.

C. Hagan, *Global Family Office Investing*,
https://doi.org/10.1007/978-3-030-18224-3_1

members and the business is sold resulting in a cash influx. Families are a core element to our security and mental stability. Apart from familial love, money does much of the same. When you combine the two you should have the utmost in safety, security, and fortification with a tinge of dysfunction. A family that talks money and manages money often stays in the money. To keep it in the family, as the old saying goes is much more to remind us of where life comes from: families that stay the course are studies in succession and transition; discipline and luck; evolution and dignity. Regardless, the simple fact remains, most of the billions are created not overnight and not in one generation, but in a succession of generations. With luck, a well-planned family office can not only provide family members with income and stability, but can help future generations achieve success in their chosen fields.

Today a family office is available to anyone who decides to establish a family office entity. Over the past decade, technology has leveled the playing field to such that forming a family office is very easy. Most offices begin as a reporting unit and advisory unit or an office in a family business, and most begin with the success of a family business or generational wealth created by a family member which is then unified around a cohesive plan.

A family office by nature is a long-term investor and they should not suffer from a fear of missing out on investments and trends. One of the key differences between someone on the street and a family office is a long-term plan that is well-defined and well-protected. If that plan calls for aggressive investment tactics, usually the aggressive tactics are piled into an appropriate vehicle, or perhaps the family sets up an alpha-driven hedge fund. Family offices have certain mandates and so funds will be allocated to particular asset classes and ventures, versus a flow of blind investment.

Establishing a family office is a conscious act meant to keep watch on the assets, organize the fortunes, and plan for the associated family and enterprises, generally passing them on to other generations. As a vehicle the family office has been used since the beginning of estate administration and management, and it was in use in ancient days, albeit under another banner. Heads of estates, earldoms, majordomos, and administrators are arguably the first; administering on behalf of the royals, noble families, ecclesiastical prices, and eventually wealthy merchants. One of the more successful examples in the English-speaking world is the landed gentry, who due to their independent means and varied skill sets migrated to managing and administering of their own estates. After all, the gentry had to stay relevant by staying wealthy first and foremost; otherwise they would lose their influence. They did not have titles or populations they could tax and local prominence could change from one family to another based on fortunes, so there was a constant scurry to

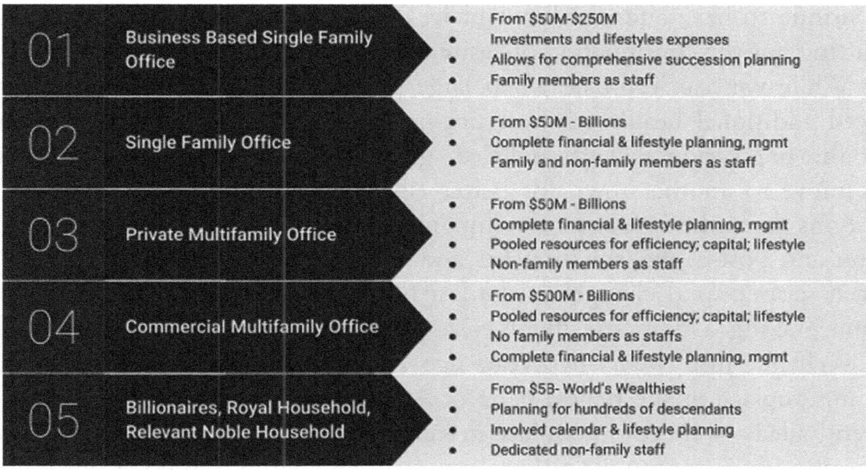

Fig. 1.1 Types of family offices

stay relevant and rich. The landed gentry used management of their holdings to hold onto power and then used profits to diversify into commercial ventures to expand their portfolios. In reality, the gentry on both sides of the Atlantic had to oversee the continuous management of enterprise and funds, and there was a responsibility to keep the family in the money (Fig. 1.1).

The Business of Inheritance: The Generational Changes Ahead

Family offices surround the core actions of succession and inheritance and it seems talk is always focused on the next generation. Often what one generation wants is completely different from what the other generation wants. This is only magnified with education and affluence. In Australia, over 90% of the next generation of family offices have different aspirations than the previous generation's aspirations.[2] In the Western world, particularly America, the generations alive today are vastly different from the last four American generations that were widely studied in America. Their spending patterns are not even on par with previous generations spending patterns. While children and parents may have common ground and many similarities—even similar upbringings—generations are different. I do not expect this to compound and widen any more than it already has, but I do expect each generation to

[2]Deloitte & The Table Club Survey (2017).

continue to have and develop a niche obfuscation of time and experience, cutting out the continuation of easily calculated mass nostalgia.

While you can estimate when large populations of people will age and need additional healthcare, you can no longer gauge when large swatches of the population will get married, get a bonus or promotion, buy cars, or move to another town for better employment. This is for a variety of reasons from the internet to a shift in global values, but also from education and post-capitalism thoughts and theories sinking in. There have also been seismic-sized changes in the last fifty years. Not even air travel is the same; taking a domestic flight costs about the same as renting a car for a weekend. Just twenty-five years ago in 1994 computers were becoming commonplace in the richest parts of America and Apple—or Macs as they were called—were commonplace in most of these schools. Emails had yet to become common; mobile phones were large and without internet capabilities and Facebook, Netflix, and Google—the most profitable companies in the last few decades—had yet to be founded. In fact, only Apple and Amazon were around in 1994 and they were more so scruffy startups than corporate empires. Vast change has occurred in a compounded manner, we have had waves of technological and structural change in the last two decades, and when you have vast change you have, quite obviously, many changes and advancements.

It is obvious that those born in 1880 will be different from those born in 1980. To put this in a wider frame—in 1760 Nicolas-Joseph Cugnot invented the first self-propelled vehicle. He spent the better part of his life in France, perfecting his invention while battling deep pocketed competition in Germany, Italy, and the United States. It wasn't until 1885 when Karl Benz patented the Benz Patent-Motorwagen that the automobile became readily available in the marketplace. In 1890 the automobile was a very big luxury and luxuries were hard to hold onto; production lines inside factories relied on commodities like rubber and metals and those were hard to come by during wartimes; if the country was at war the commodities went to the troops. Such realities are no longer commonplace.

Establishing that there is change ahead with future generations, one can begin to plan and focus on the bigger picture. This is important to understand for planning and succession matters. There is change in every generation and as one can expect families often disagree. While many can work past issues, many are unable to move forward and a consensus must be made. Many times the best option is to make separate accommodations for the feuding family members. One can think of such an arrangement as a "carve out" allowing for the assets to be split and set up in however many smaller pieces that need to be set up. It has been said that the famous painter Lucian Freud, OM—the grandson of Sigmund—was so entrenched in hatred with his brother Clement from a childhood prank that they spent most of their lives never talking. A family office cannot support dysfunction and expect to carry on with independence or efficiency. That said, it is not untold for family members to have their shares bought out by other family members or to split family offices and family foundations to accommodate new households and to limit sparing between family members. I cover more of this in Chapter 7.

As to be expected, the story of a family office is as unique as the family itself. Family offices are the latest type of financial entity to take on wealth managers, hedge funds, private equity shops, and blue blooded investment bankers. One of the major reasons is terms of investment. Not needing to take high incomes and exit the investment in a five-year horizon, family offices have stepped into the game and have been developing a deep bench of talent and have the ability to poach from the world's finest financial institutions.

At this moment the family office is one of the more talked about forms of asset management, planning, and succession planning. As I will discuss through this book, the concept of family offices is routed in European history, and apart from the United States and China, many family offices are still located in continental Europe. The United Kingdom, France, Germany, and Italy hold the titles for having the most family offices, and they also have some of the oldest continually managed family-owned concerns outside of royal households. However, the future of family offices is not in the growth forecasts of Europe, the future of family offices lies in the hands of Asia Pacific where the concept of a family office is still in its infancy and many are forming as family office funds and as single family office shops for single beneficiaries.

What is the point of family offices? In many ways it is to organize. A family office, whether it is a single family office or a multifamily office, strives to accomplish what it cannot accomplish with traditional vendors; a comprehensive fiduciary organization that manages all aspects of accounting and finance, investment, real estate, lifestyle, and legacies such as family foundations, succession, and generational inheritance.

Last, a question I am asked frequently is how much wealth a family needs to have in order to establish a family office. There is no simple answer. There is no concrete financial amount required to form a family office. In reality any amount of wealth that is to be passed down to heirs should be contained in a privately held company, a trust, a foundation, or a family office. In reality a family office entity can be set up without any assets, as family offices tend to operate as reporting and advisory units; if the family office manages assets directly and wants to integrate portfolio companies under one organization, one can simply form an umbrella organization and transfer the majority of shares to the holding company.

Bibliography

Deloitte & The Table Club Survey (2007).

2

Family Office History

Family Office History—North America

The history of economics and trade is one filled with associated family interests. Today the story of a family office almost always begins with the success of a family business, or a family member sets forth a goal to unify the wealth and assets to safeguard and cohesively plan the management and deployment of the assets in custody. Perhaps they plan to pass it along to the family, perhaps they aspire for a purpose built museum. That development depends on the heirs, industry, and assets. Often as family offices make do for heirs and their particular interests they begin to involve the next generation completely (Fig. 2.1).

In North America family offices in the nineteenth and twentieth centuries centered on businesses built by single entrepreneurs and family members who began to plan for future generations and over time participated in systematic asset diversification. They were also aided by immigration and wealthy families transitioning to America and bringing their financial acumen with them. Many of these family offices originated in the Northern cities of Boston, New York City, and Philadelphia.

Large pools of capital and fortunes made by the likes of the Astor, Guggenheim, Rockefeller, or Bessemer families were as much experiments in capitalism as they were chance encounters with industry and society, resulting in unfounded wealth. Over time the fortunes added up, with some paying particular interest to generating the largest of fortunes. Rockefeller and Morgan created a network of trusts concealing ownership in companies

C. Hagan, *Global Family Office Investing*,
https://doi.org/10.1007/978-3-030-18224-3_2

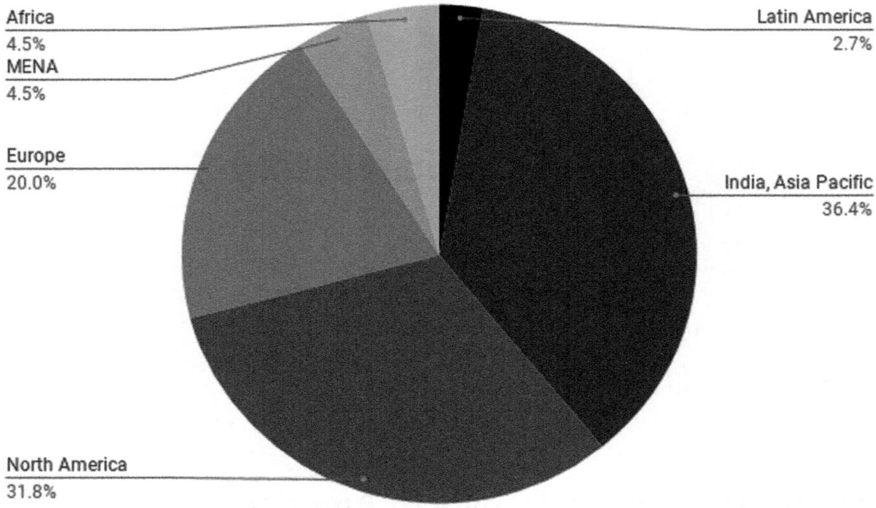

Fig. 2.1 Where are the rich?

and partnerships. This led to the term antitrust and trust busting, as officials banded together to bust the trusts, thereby eliminating unfair competition. The funds generated were so severe and robust they ended up in trust companies overseen by sophisticated organizations compiled of attorneys, bankers, and management professionals for the sole intention of solidifying the family fortune for the heirs. Managers did everything from creating trust funds in the classic sense (to hold property for the benefit of another) to picking single name equities for investment speculation to financing ventures and establishing mortgages for family members. These professionals and managers worked for the capital at hand and the capital was in-house. It was permanent. It is debated between J.P. Morgan, Henry Phipps, Jr., and John D. Rockefeller as to who organized the first American family office solely devoted to managing family funds. Regardless, these family office ventures proved successful and efficient and a new type of money management was born in the United States: the single family office. Many families followed—again largely Northern and New England financial families—and over time some of these organizations became modern-day multifamily offices like Northern Trust, Bessemer Trust, Boston's North American Management, and the newly rebranded Rockefeller Capital.

Apart from fortunes generated in the aforementioned style many family offices inherited the operations and ethos of continental European style family offices. Indeed a great many of these families emigrated from Europe, and with them they brought the practices of dynastic succession to a new country steeped deep in the idea of building a better future for you and your family. That meant leaving offspring and descendants with an inheritance. More than often it meant combining business interests or taking on family members as partners. In America, during the turn of the centuries, a great deal of enterprises adopted the affixture of brothers or sons in their names including a few of the oldest financial institutions in America: Brown Brothers Harriman[1] (1818) and Alex. Brown & Sons (1800).

In the American major capitals of Boston, New York City, and Baltimore many were well versed in economic matters and international trade. Families owned docks and ships and traded as far off as Asia. Eastern families were ship owners and traders, often at the forefront of physical trade. The first American international trading companies originated out of Massachusetts, Rhode Island, and Connecticut—not a far reach from where the first American family offices originated. This mimicked "merchant adventurer" behavior in Europe and included all types of Americans including a lot of sons from America's gentry like FDR's grandfather, Warren Delano, Jr, who was employed with Russell & Company in modern-day Guangzhou, formerly of the Canton system. This type of trading was arbitrage at its finest. Market information flowed freely in these economic capitals, and risk pooled together to syndicate investments deemed too risky for one to burden alone. It was high stakes and families were the insiders. Early on families benefited from government affiliation—both from elected and appointed perspectives—and in many ways the North East particularly states like New York mimicked the European hierarchy of aristocratic privilege complete with country estates and patents from royals.

Outside the eastern and coastal capitals families focused on building supply and service outposts and vertically integrating their already established businesses, originally in agriculture and manufacturing but soon in oil fields, logistics terminals, dry goods—including West Indies rum—and early concoctions of chemicals and aggregates. In Chicago and Wisconsin brewing, food manufacturing and developments in packaging and consumer goods created enormous collections of wealth—as did market trading—all in the hands of families. With every Wrigley there was sure to be countless smaller industry barons, and that was just in Chicago. Minneapolis, Detroit, and Toronto had similar stories with intersecting regional industry and entrepreneurial endeavors establishing some of the best known American

[1]Reflecting the merger of Harriman Brothers & Co. (1931) and Brown Bros. & Co. (1818) the founders of which were from the same family as the founders of Alex. Brown & Sons and Brown, Shipley & Co.

companies in history, as well as countless middle market enterprises, family fortunes, and small business enterprises.

Minneapolis and Chicago connected the west to the east in addition to serving as regional capitals of industry as the American population expanded west. The area now known as California was listed as an island on nearly every major map and Atlas in Europe into the eighteenth century. The Lower Mainland region of British Columbia—Greater Vancouver today—was a well-known trading area for indigenous peoples and the fur trade but like San Francisco and Los Angeles development would lag behind until the mid-century gold rush led populations to the west. In due time the mid-1800s arrived and the western part of North America flourished. The population increased by over 300% in California alone and that put the region in a constant flow of supply and demand.

As the Western states developed so did a well-trodden trading enterprise between the cities of Los Angeles, San Francisco, Portland, and Seattle. Domestic trade was soon joined by international trade from Asia and Asian–American family-owned businesses increased including immigrants from China, Korea, and Malaysia. Some of this wealth was highly influential and incredibly vast, from the Heart family and Getty family to modern-day Western barons like Bill Gates, Patrick Soon-Shiong, and Eli Broad. These billionaires no doubt have family offices, but getting rich off a moonshot or creating billions in one generation is not the way it is usually done. Not to detour any attempts at moonshots, but going from zero to one billion is rarely done. Going from zero to one million, ten million to one hundred million to one billion is done often, compared to the opposite. It is much more palatable and realistic for families to move and emigrate, or to expand, reinvest, and develop the original business, either within the same entity or other entities created to expand. It is in the latter that we find a more relatable situation in the creation of a family office inside a growing family-owned enterprise.

In theory, the American Kennedy Family has retained a substantial amount of wealth from the original Joseph P. Kennedy's day, and today the wealth is in trusts, investment holdings, foundations, and real estate. The family still owns 4 acres next to the merchandise mart, the latter was sold years ago but the family retained ownership of Wolf Point, a prominent parcel of land next to the mart. They have been codeveloping the land with Hines, the Houston-based developer. In the merchandise mart sale to Vornado, the Kennedys were rumored to have used a UPREIT which stands for: umbrella partnership real estate investment trust. This security allows the transfer of appreciated property to descendants tax-free, even more so in trusts. By this move alone the

Kennedy's have been able to keep their fortune well intact for future generations. However, many have praised the use of trusts by the patriarch Joseph P. Kennedy. It just so happened that in the elder Kennedy's day the richest of the rich used trusts and established foundations and family offices. Kennedy, a former stockbroker at Boston-based Hayden, Stone & Co., clearly learned estate planning from the best and brightest.

An Older History

The administration of royal purses and lands, horses and soldiers, crown jewels, and family holdings required a single administrator or a group of administrators handling the treasury. The majordomo or head of house, maybe even the exchequer—this is when it first began in Europe. In many ways it has yet to change.

To develop a concise grasp on global family office history one must look to the beginning of human markets and mercantile consumption within semi-developed cities in the Mediterranean, Middle East, and Inner Asia area. A difference must be noted between kingdoms and domains over enterprise and trade. The first trade was the food trade, more specifically the grain trade. Whatever the day and age of history you can most surely count on an enterprising family sailing the high seas to supply goods needed for trade; sending sons afar to run foreign operations; or marrying daughters off to strengthen business ties. These merchant families became very wealthy from trade and gained power as they developed into merchant global traders, complete with ships and independent soldiers.

In Asia, content with being cut off from the rest of the world, we have the precursors to modern futures exchanges in the form of physical rice exchanges. Everything was moved by boat. In Japan, rice settled payments, much like salt and gold later in history. In Osaka, right outside the former capital Kyoto, commodity markets flourished and an influential system developed into a shadow banking system based on rice trading and rice futures. Ties to ancestors and ancient commerce is very much the normal route in Japan, with the oldest operating company in the world, Kongō Gumi Co., Ltd., rumored to have been founded in 578 and still active as a subsidiary of Takamatsu Corporation of Japan.

Meanwhile in Europe

Trade between Japan and Europe is linked to the Portuguese in the sixteenth century. If in doubt look no further than to tempura, a Japanese staple which has its roots in Portuguese cuisine. Regardless, the earliest days of European trade were dominated by the Venetians. But for history's sake they were soon replaced by the Medici family who were to rule for centuries and establish additional cultural and finance centers, as well as provide ecclesiastical heirs for the Vatican. As with the Medici's in Italy, the Rothschild's had a very tight grip across multiple countries in continental Europe for a number of centuries. The family financed governments during wars and made investments during times of early technological innovation resulting in profits from railroads, mining and other heavy industry, aside from the industries they initially prospered in which was lending, commodity trading, and international development. Eventually the family became fabulously wealthy and culturally illustrious in all of aristocratic Europe, while maintaining the vast Rothschild banking enterprise on multiple continents.

In the United Kingdom there exists a perfect example of an active and successful family office, the Duchy of Cornwall. The Duchy of Cornwall was established for the eldest son of the monarch. The duchy is a crown body and that prevents the duchy from having to pay tax though Charles, Prince of Wales, pays a voluntary fee each year to subdue controversy. In this duchy, there are abnormal rights, rights that we could only expect a European royal to have such as rights to wreckage, jus naufragii (right of shipwreck), off the Cornish coast.

The sovereign formerly controlled the entire state and decided every matter. This has since changed, but the framework of the old system still exists, the only difference is that it is for the country and dominions of the United Kingdom versus the royal family. With that said a worthwhile example of third-party administration of family finances can be found in the "Green Cloth" files. The Board of Green Cloth contained officers. The officers of the green cloth all wore green, and by order of power held the following: the Lord Steward (Chairman); Treasurer of the Household; Comptroller of the Household; Cofferer of the Household (which was removed in 1782); and the Masters of the Household. The latter was the operation unit, much like a Chief Operating Officer in a modern corporation, who oversees multiple company departments:

> Officers of the Green Cloth; Board of Green Cloth
>
> Lord Steward: The office of steward of the household customarily designated that of lord steward was in the gift of the crown. The lord steward was the

> principal officer of the household below stairs in whom was vested the bulk of the patronage in that department.
>
> Treasurer: The office of Treasurer of the Household had its origin in that of Keeper of the Wardrobe of the Household by which he was occasionally known even after 1485. The Treasurer ranked second after the Lord Steward and entered office on receiving a staff and taking an oath. The office was held by commoners except for the years 1603–18 and 1641–5 when it was occupied by peers. If not already a privy counsellor, the Treasurer was admitted to the council as a matter of course on appointment.[2]

Just below treasurer was comptroller and below comptroller was cofferer. The word coffer means a chest or perhaps a box, or in this case a chest that held valuables like gold and silver coins. As listed above they often promoted from within until this was handed over to the peers. As the royal household parted from directly controlling the government, so did their finances and what was considered a family asset was separate from what was considered a state asset. However, that is not with our complication, agreements, and ongoing management and stewardship of the asset. If a family has assets to manage and if they wish to maintain ownership of those assets, someone must consciously manage them or they will be lost, sold, or mismanaged and suffer a similar fate.

If you take England for instance and the royals, titled aristocrats and untitled but highly pedigreed upper classes from a historical perspective the branches of the family trees come from the same confluences. You see a historical pattern of elites merging with other elites to form super elites, who are largely hereditary peers or hereditary princes and princesses, in addition to out-of-wedlock offspring, affairs, and surrogates and second- and third-born sons with nothing but adventure and the ability to underwrite activity. In England the surname FitzRoy is an old Anglo-Norman name meaning "son of the king" and in many instances it was given to an out-of-wedlock son or daughter of a king, mostly the decedents of Charles II and his many mistresses but also with three daughters by Henry I and also pertaining to the modern duke, Henry Oliver Charles FitzRoy, 12th Duke of Grafton, descendant of Henry FitzRoy, 1st Duke of Richmond and Somerset who was the son of Henry VIII and his mistress Elizabeth Blount. While dizzying, it is a serious part of history. It was not uncommon for heirs to ensure they had heirs and spares; heirs including heirs from surrogates outside the marriages. This makes for an interesting family tree. As you delve deeper into Europe you find a culture rife with princes, royal households, and their offshoots—a

[2]Officers of the Green Cloth, Institute of Historical Research, SOAS, University of London.

basketful of wealthy families, dynasties, and medieval age inheritances pared with entrepreneurial and financial fortunes.

In England, the landed gentry were a force to reckon with from an early start. During Britain's agricultural heyday you didn't need a title to be a gentleman, just a country estate and some arable land. Even if the gentry were a step below the higher echelons of Britain's upper classes, they were still a part of the upper class and held tremendous social influence over the British upper middle class and middle class. They differ from the American version of upper middle class in the sense that they have substantial lineage. Another difference would be their inheritance model which mimicked that of the nobility and is far different from the equal inheritance tradition practiced in America which puts a damper on dynastic dreams in any grand imperial form. To add to this, a good amount of the landed gentry were descendants of the more powerful and esteemed aristocratic families, royal nobles, or unrecognized royal family members who were born out of wedlock. This class produced countless politicians from the represented lands, and since voting rights were historically tied to land, the system was near impossible to break apart. Parliament was overwhelmingly represented by the gentry until reform came to Britain in the mid-nineteenth century. Historian David Cannadine summarized the landed gentry's lack of concern for being untitled class since they were "the equivalent of continental nobles[3]" due to lifestyle, connections, and wealth. They also produced much of their wealth from landholdings and thus owned the means of production (income from rents, farming estates, livestock, brewing). The untitled gentry of Britain owned most of the economics until perhaps the biggest bluster in the entire system occurred by way of the industrial revolution which outplayed British agricultural wealth with the onslaught of cheaper prices, free trading from industrial developments.

Guilds were influential in Europe, particularly in England and Italy. Guilds and guildhalls were central to trade and commerce in most cities for the laboring gentry and commoners, which accounted for most of the population in medieval Europe. In the United Kingdom, specifically London, you were unable to conduct business if you were not a member of a guild. These guilds developed into livery companies which are still in existence today in London.

[3]"Class in Britain", David Cannadine, Penguin, March 30, 2000.

Bibliography

See history of Harriman Brothers Company and history of Brown Bros. & Co., both American private banking and finance companies.
See Officers of The Green Cloth, Officers of the Green Cloth, Institute of Historical Research, SOAS, University of London.
Cannadine, David, "Class in Britain." Penguin Books Limited, London, England. 2000.

3

Europe

Many of the world's great fortunes have come from the United States but the grandest inheritances have often been from Europe. The system that prevails: male-line primogeniture—holds that the first-born legitimate son is to inherit his parent's assets. While this is not as commonplace as before, inheritance is complicated in the European area when titles and hereditary assets are considered (Fig. 3.1).

While the story of Europe is one of prosperity it is a story of one entrenched in battle, steeped in history with plenty of legends, the parts that have not been amalgamated have always seemed to escape stronger in their unity. One of the first banding of countries together in a supranational form—the European Coal and Steel Community (ECSC) which was founded in 1951 and a precursor to the European Union—was established to regulate industrial supply and demand systems. Above all the idea was to avoid continued damage to industrial utilities during wars. This morphed into the European Union today. Not only does Europe lend its name to the ultimate control of centuries of discovery and trade, but also to the concept of nation states grouping together to create the ultimate state power. Europe is deeply international and in this chapter I will attempt to cohesively illuminate international operations in the single family office and multifamily office space.

C. Hagan, *Global Family Office Investing*,
https://doi.org/10.1007/978-3-030-18224-3_3

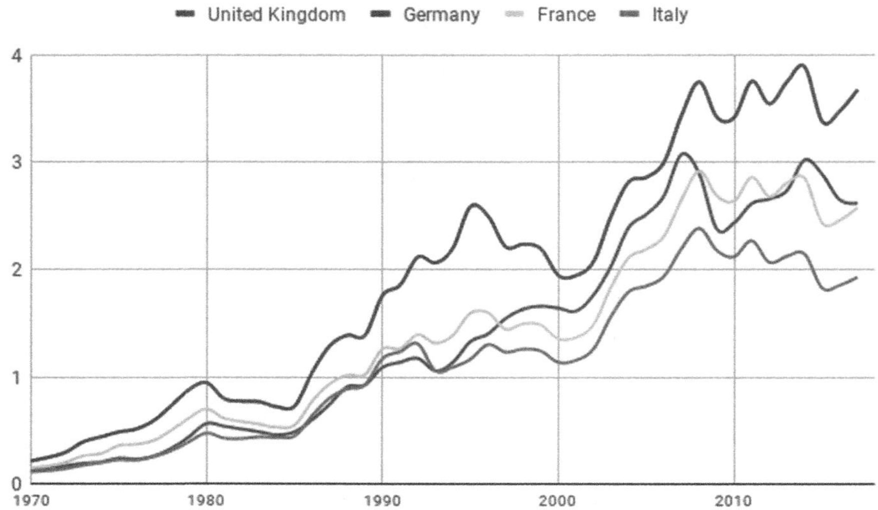

Fig. 3.1 European GDP World Bank

Single Family Offices

Single family offices (SFOs) have been going about in Europe for a long time albeit under a different name. Royals are at the top as their wealth has largely been derived from estates and investment holdings over the past century as income from taxation stopped. In England there are marvelous examples with the existence of the Duchy of Lancaster and Duchy of Cornwall which serve the sovereign and the sovereign's heir. It should be noted that these are not part of The Crown Estate, which is a special corporation body that holds properties that belong to the institution of the monarchy and not the monarch's personal estate, with revenue and income from the Crown going to the Her Majesty's Treasury (also known as HM Treasury or the Exchequer) for the nations use in exchange from funding the civil government. While it all sounds quite confusing, it is rather simple. The Crown Estate is a non-statutory corporation sole that acts within the United Kingdom's commonwealth realms, and includes assets historically linked to the monarch, but no longer in the monarch's personal possessions. The assets of the two Duchy's belong to the title and the heir of the titles.

From an estate planning perspective the royal estate in the United Kingdom, the Duchy of Lancaster and the Duchy of Cornwall, are possibly the best examples of holding a vast fortune in trust, while allowing for reinvestment and planning for continued growth. Both were founded hundreds of years ago, both are technically private estates and both exist to serve British sovereigns. The Duchy of Cornwall was created for Edward, The Prince of Wales (often referred to as Edward, The Black Prince). Despite a few changes, its royal charter has stayed intact and the Duchy of Cornwall provides Prince Charles with most of his income and most of Prince Williams's income. Here land rights extend to river beds and seashore, the duchy owns most of the riverbeds and foreshore, which is the in-between of the high tide and low tide marks, surrounding the region of Cornwall and the Isles of Scilly which lie at the bottom tip of England in Cornwall. This is just one portfolio of the duchy as the duchy is not only based in Cornwall, but holds estates all over the world and is active in the management of those businesses and estates.

The ancient Lancaster inheritance, which is also known as the Duchy of Lancaster, was formed in 1265. The Duchy of Lancaster is the British sovereign's vehicle, and in this case held in trust for the office that Queen Elizabeth holds. The duchy pays out income from holdings to the current king or queen. The landholdings produce rents derived from the various estates:

> The Duchy of Lancaster is a private estate owned by Her Majesty The Queen, as Duke of Lancaster. The rural estates consist of 18,484 hectares of land in England and Wales and comprise commercial, agricultural and residential properties, the majority of which are in Lancashire, Yorkshire, Cheshire, Staffordshire and Lincolnshire. Additionally the Duchy has a significant commercial property portfolio largely in the Savoy precinct off the Strand in London, a portfolio of financial investments and a small urban residential portfolio.[1]

Under the Crown Lands Act 1702 it was decided that the sovereign would receive income not capital from the Duchy. This also accounts for any sales that take place and according to the guidance of the Duchy Council, capital is reinvested in landholdings or developments. Apart from that, royal funds are held in accounts at Coutts, which is a private bank that traces its origins to the year 1692. Coutts has been owned by National Westminster Bank (NatWest) since 1920, but has enjoyed a history with the royal family and aristocracy of Britain for hundreds of years.

Europe has a history of private banking second to none. As mentioned in the last chapter, many European families immigrated to American during the wars. With them they bought forward their traditions. The families who stayed behind fled to neutral territories or cities which promised freedom. From there they continued their practice. It is almost always the case that a financial or trade-oriented family sets forth family offices to take advantage of

[1] Duchy of Lancaster Official Documents.

centralization, planning, and opportunism to provide for heirs. You will find families in continental Europe who state that they have had a "family office" in the form of an administrator which dealt with the family-held estates and finances long before family offices were popular. I will go into more historical details later in this book, but those families and professionals are largely correct. Administrators and then private bankers (within Switzerland, or one of the cultural capitals) handled duties. They went beyond the normal duties of any banker we have known in the modern era, apart from a Swiss private banker in the truest sense.

Multifamily Offices

Stonehage Fleming was formed with Fleming Family Partners, having merged in 2015. Before that both companies held similar administrative and industry duties in the family office spectrum but had different histories. Stonehage was established in the 1970s to provide investors and families with trust and wealth services. The Fleming Family was formed after the sale of Flemings to Chase Manhattan. The Fleming family had a few noted successes, most importantly the profits from the sale of Flemings to Chase, but also the 007 copyrights to Ian Fleming's literary franchise. One of the ways Stonehage excels in their bank-oriented MFO model is by having multiple branches for services. They are an international family office system. Perhaps the best example of an international MFO framework, complete with branches, events, and all types of planning expertise.

MFOs are not always part of banks or commercial financial companies; often MFOs are a grouping of families grouped together for office resources or a grouping of family resources due to familial relations. In the last decade the US market has seen a move of smaller RIA firms pivoting from the HNW market to that of the UHNW market, choosing to handle a select number of wealthy families in a boutique fashion, pooling together resources and opportunities.

Trusts

It would not be fair to the professional to leave out the mention of trusts in European family offices. Irish Trust law is very similar to English Trust law, but more common law based. This is mainly governed by the Trustee Act of 1893, and subsequent developments. Income tax from activities is only liable to taxation of the Trustees residence. If the trustee is in a no tax zone there will be no trust income tax. Both benefit from the shared common law structure. Trusts and trust law in Europe is complicated and well-developed but they technically only exist in countries with common law. That limits the choices to the United Kingdom and UK domiciles. Despite the common law and civil law disconnect, many European centers are hubs for trust management and fiduciary services, it just may be that the assets are owned by a company domiciled in a common law state. The United Kingdom also has the Channel Islands which function as independent governments with separate company and tax law. The islands of Jersey and Guernsey in the Channel Islands are well-known Crown dependent tax havens; however, they cooperate with the authorities. There was a time when many of the offshore jurisdictions in the world—particularly the leading centers—refused to cooperate with authorities.

In Europe one tends to be international, even if by accident. The close borders and economic cooperation make sense for one to use various jurisdictions. This is particularly important if you are setting up trusts and foundations as many countries in Europe have shifting tax policies. If a grantor is setting up trusts to provide income for his children, grandchildren, and great-grandchildren that live in France, he will likely be advised to use Switzerland and another favorable country to base his assets and network of trusts. While this system has been blamed for inequality, it is prudent to regard location of one's registered holdings, tax status, citizenship, and the disbursement of trust income.

While there are many types of trusts, let's briefly discuss the most popular types according to Companies House, the United Kingdom's registrar of companies. In my opinion it is important we utilize common law over civil law, as common law has well-defined trust law and property law as well as the legal principle of precedent, where judges consider previous case law decisions into their decisions.

Bare Trusts

Assets in a bare trust are held in the name of a trustee. However, the beneficiary has the right to all of the capital and income of the trust at any time if they're 18 or over (in England and Wales), or 16 or over (in Scotland). This means the assets set aside by the settlor will always go directly to the intended beneficiary.

Discretionary Trusts

These are where the trustees can make certain decisions about how to use the trust income, and sometimes the capital.

Accumulation Trusts

This is where the trustees can accumulate income within the trust and add it to the trust's capital. They may also be able to pay income out, as with discretionary trusts.

Mixed Trusts

These are a combination of more than one type of trust. The different parts of the trust are treated according to the tax rules that apply to each part.

Settlor-Interested Trusts

These are where the settlor or their spouse or civil partner benefits from the trust. The trust could be: an interest-in-possession trust, an accumulation trust, or a discretionary trust.

Non-resident Trusts

This is a trust where the trustees are not residents in the United Kingdom for tax purposes.

Continental Europe

It is not unusual to find a centuries-old family company in Europe. On that same note it is not unusual to meet a European from a grand background without the fortune or associated riches. Fortunes have been fractured as have art collections and cultural collections, torn apart from war and political upheaval or from gambling, or dysfunction or time.

These types of offices were built around the initial business fortune or passed on from generation to generation in a semi-aristocratic manner; industry shared and carved out might eventually eclipse the original fortune. From that you had a vast cadre of types of family office—from trust funds dispersions to heirs using fortunes for business matters and commercial endeavors. As the American system is at times a semi-inheritance the European system often was gilded and multitiered, with merchants utilizing wealth to overcome racial boundaries. Of course, Europe being Europe many of these merchant families elevated to the aristocratic echelons over time or simply married into them.

Success in Europe has always been different than other parts of the world. A grand puzzle of countries and cultures, continental Europe has a dense population with a developed infrastructure and multiple booming economic centers. Royalty and the aristocracy is part of the lifeblood in Europe and fortunes are often intertwined within royal households. Historically in Germany, Italy, and North Europe there was a mix of secular and religious princes, junkers, and ducals. You really couldn't operate without the local grandee sponsoring you. Additionally a smattering of offshore jurisdictions competing throughout Europe enabled fortunes to be hidden and stowed away safely—for better or for worse—but regardless, establishing some of the best estate planning and asset transferring systems in the world. Older tax havens like the Channel Islands, Luxembourg, and Liechtenstein, and new tax zones and tax-efficient areas like Dublin and other parts of Ireland are still in use.

Families think very long term in Europe—longer than those in the United States—this transcends into the structures of European families. Professionals have gone to great lengths to establish a robust system. Trade and geographic artisan endeavors made Europe a haven for businesses and a large number of very old businesses owned by family, their holding companies, or groups of shareholders persist in existence. Europe is also made out of tax shelters. Malta is one of the most important havens available, sitting only beside Luxembourg, Switzerland, Liechtenstein, and the Channel Islands. Home to a stock exchange and numerous banks including Lombard Bank Malta, HSBC Bank Malta, Bank of Valletta, and APS (Figs. 3.2 and 3.3).

Austria, Switzerland, Luxembourg, and Liechtenstein: Funds often end up here. Luxembourg is considered a fund capital of the world, if not the fund capital of the world. Trust law is developing, like Switzerland but their lies a strong history of custodian and fiduciary rules. China has been developing stronger relationships with Luxembourg over the past decade. Luxembourg is very stable, with public debt hovering around 20% and a AAA credit rating.

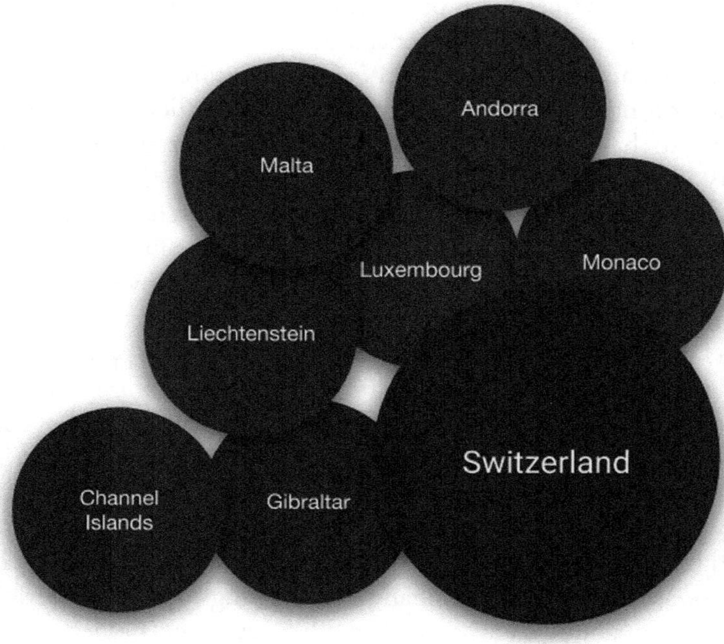

Fig. 3.2 Where are Europe's family offices?

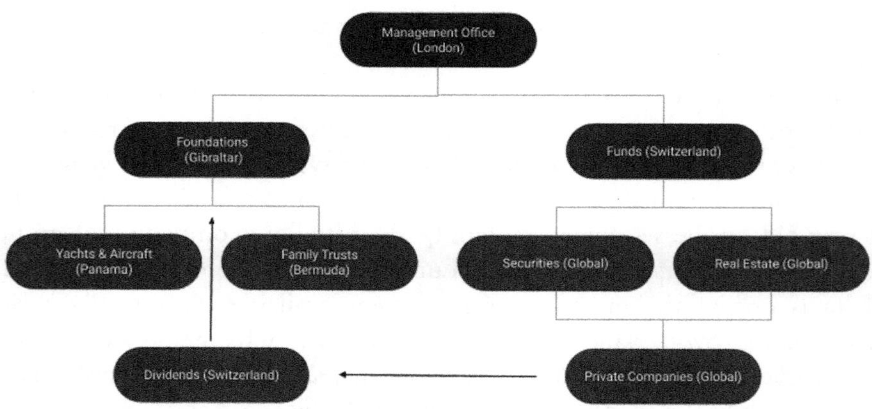

Fig. 3.3 European family office structure example

The economy is well diversified the financial sector makes up over 25% of the market. It should be noted that Luxembourg takes tremendous pride in the capitalization of their financial institutions.

Long a bastion of private baking, much like the banking in Switzerland, Lichtenstein is focused on private banking which encompasses a tremendous amount of bespoke services. Additionally, finance accounts for a sizable majority of Lichtenstein's economy and revenue. The princely Liechtenstein Global Trust (LGT), which is the largest family controlled asset management business in Europe, employs close to 4000 people in 20 countries. It is predominantly owned by Prince of Liechtenstein Foundation, which holds an estimated $6–7B in assets including securities and company shares, but also including cultural holdings and diverse operations such as communications for the royal family and princely houses. HSH Prince Constantin is the CEO of Foundation Prince Liechtenstein, and runs the foundation companies and operations.

As Austria tends to be the foothold and capital of Central and Eastern Europe, Austrian banks hold assets in Central Europe and Eastern Europe. Historically the capitals of Austria controlled and managed the wealth brought in by the associated trade surrounding the Danube River which twists through Hungary, Serbia, Romania, and Bulgaria before hitting the Black Sea. Austria has been at the core of European business since the fifteenth century. Largely ruled by the Hapsburgs of Austro-Hungarian fame, who in turn made a few families fabulously wealthy including the Fuggers of Augsburg and Rothschild's.

The Austrian branch of the Rothschild family and their firm Credit-Anstalt (founded in 1855) in particular orchestrated an elaborate system of ownership and control which benefited the family for a very long time. This included vast holdings across the former Austro-Hungarian Empire and an unusual hold on Europe's great industries and playgrounds, resulting in unfounded power throughout academia, commerce, culture, and art. While the Rothschild family is diverse and scattered throughout the world the story of the firm, at his time styled as Credit-Anstalt, is a major mark in history. Credit-Anstalt was a banking house which was heavily invested in Austrian companies, Austrian banks, and Central and Eastern European company shares, loans, and assets. When loans began to crumble by the Rothschild-dominated Viennese banking system created a ripple effect reaching all across Europe and into the former Ottomon Empire. In 1931 Credit-Anstalt declared that it had lost more than half of its capital; the Rothschild's Austrian financial reign was over but the family still held untold riches in Austria. Recently a forest land sale in Austria highlighted the former grip the Rothschild had on Imperial Austria, the family heirs Geoffrey Huget and Nancy Tilghman unloaded an inherited forest estate named "Langau" for some

$100M. The estate spans over 5000 hectares and includes two power stations, a ski area, and a few hunting lodges.

To add to this history, Austria is very friendly with Russia. Austria's Raiffeisen International receives substantial revenue from their Russia operations and apart from the shared Jewish history and deep Jewish culture present in Austria and Russia, it is without a shadow of a doubt a deep banking relationship from the days of Soviet occupation. Austria has been implicated in the Russian Laundromat Scandal—a heist of some $80B in funds—a scandal involving the looting of state funds when Russia first opened up for foreign business. Whether or not that is true is another matter, but the case remains that Russian billions are in Austrian banks and we will likely see Russian family offices develop with more frequency in Austria.

Neutrality has its spoils and one of those is the vast expansion of commerce that neutrality allows. Long the leader in private banking, safe keeping, and custody of assets and trustee service, Switzerland is still number one. If you want a James Bond type of banking secrecy you can find it in Switzerland, complete with mountain vaults accessible only by helicopter. It just depends on what type of client you are. The three largest banks are UBS, Credit Suisse, and Julia Bar. The main hubs for business are reflected on their geographic location, resulting in Geneva for French language; Zurich for German; and Lugano for Italian. The private banks, Mirabaud and Pictet, both based in Geneva, still offer best-in-class Swiss-style private banking. It is worth noting that private banking in Switzerland began in the late 1700s in St. Gallen, merely a handful of kilometers away from Liechtenstein. Most family offices in Europe have a Swiss connection whether it is a trustee or a Swiss holding company or merely a bank account.

A more robust rival is the Swiss bank Pictet, who keeps a low profile and manages the finances of about 80 families, but is very capable with a global staff of over 4000 specialists and close to 30 branch locations. Organized as Banque Pictet et Cie SA, the group has an AUM of over 400B CHF and was formed in 1805. The bank is run by a group of eight, and at times they are well presented by the still active Pictet family. The store of Pictet has been studied and reported on for over a century, but the Witten Institute has published two editions of reports covering Banque Pictet and their operations:

> The link to the extended Pictet family is closer than might be expected, given the formal distance. According to Ivan Pictet, there is no shortage of suitable offspring waiting in the wings. In this respect, the family may be considered to have privileged access, making itself available to the company as a resource. A suitably qualified Pictet always has the option of joining the firm. However,

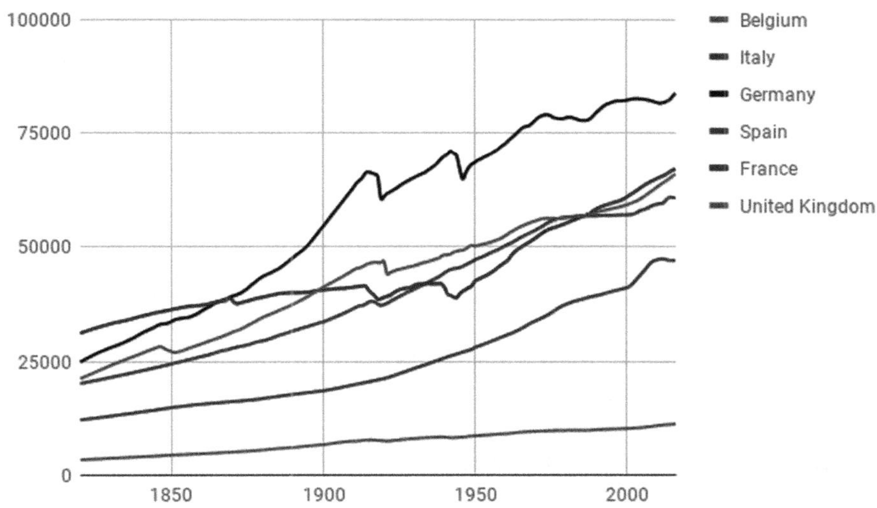

Fig. 3.4 Europe GDP purchasing power

the family aspect is restricted by the unwritten rule that a father and son or two siblings cannot be Partners at the same time.. And to further reduce the likelihood of emotional complications, the Partners from the Pictet family must be chosen by the non-family members among the Partners. In general, the Partners bearing the Pictet name have the same rights and obligations as the others. Their partnership, and thus their entitlement to a share in the company profits, is restricted to the period they remain with the company. It ends once they leave the Group. Furthermore, their offspring are never automatically entitled to become a Partner; they too have to be suitably qualified. In all this time, the organisational structures have obviously evolved, with a greater understanding of the co-evolutionary unit of a family-like partnership and a business. The model that has emerged and survived to this day is one that almost perfectly resolves the paradox that arises from the different rules of play associated with a family and a business organisation."[2] (Figs. 3.4, and 3.5)

The Business of Inheritance

Italy is home to a number of storied families and family offices, as well as family-controlled businesses. One example is Beretta. Beretta remains constant at 500 years old. The family company has extended to safety training

[2]The Pictet Model, Witten Institute for Family Business, May 2017.

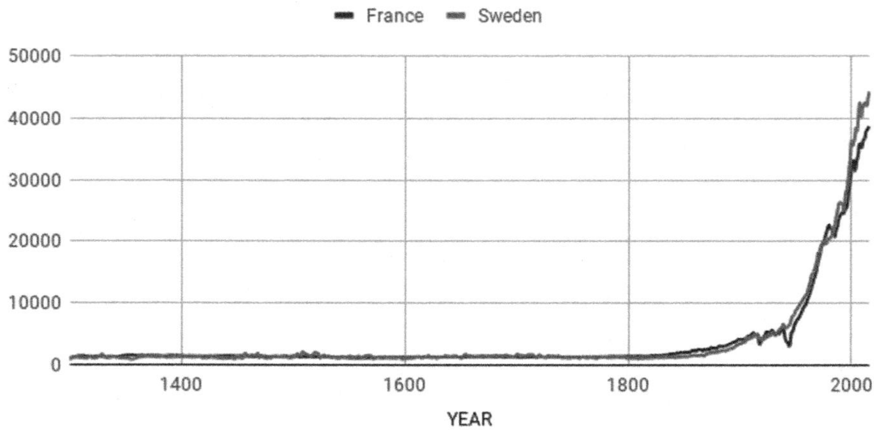

Fig. 3.5 Europe oldest national accounts

and positioned themselves as leaders in their trade with very few competitors, other than competitors in product. This is exceedingly rare—especially in firearms—as tides turn and the Beretta family has been able to ride the changes in firearms for a half millennia. Another modern example of a European giant is Lego which was formed in 1932. Kirkbi is the family office of the founding Kristiansen family and owns a substantial portion of Lego Enterprise and controls the Lego Foundation. There are international in the truest form.

From a more approachable continental royal try this: A German hereditary price with a handful of castles, two sons one of which is a minor price, a medium-sized brewery and some forest holdings dating back to 1800; or perhaps a newer fortune made from a multigenerational business recently sold to a major competitor. The prince sets up a system of family offices to handle the crown prices estate, the castle and to provide for his second son. The hereditary son takes the entitled assets but the second son takes the business enterprises and nonroyal landholdings.

Europe is built of dynasties, both historical and modern. It is also built of offshore zones and low tax zones. Monaco is still in existence and they are very relevant in the family office world, but more so to the billionaires. Europe largely made the private banking and family office model used today so it is no wonder there is tremendous longevity despite the historical friction. It is hardly unusual to stumble upon a two-hundred-year-old family business in Europe.

As mentioned, the old model and the model that prevails—primogeniture—gives all of the fortune to the eldest heir. Primogeniture detonates any idea of a fair inheritance and estate planning, despite recent efforts to move away from male-only heirs. The system keeps the assets intact by avoiding fragmentation but those who lose are the extended children. In England, illiquid male heirs have been known to make due for sisters and extended family members, sometimes by selling household art and antiques, but that is not always the case.

Case Study: The Agnelli Investment in PartnerRe

The Angellis family investment vehicle Exor, is owned by the family which numbers more than 100 descendants of the founder.

The Amsterdam-based holding company, Giovanni Agnelli BV, holds shares in Exor and in turn is held by numerous extended family member's families and their families including Umberto Agnelli, Giovanni Nasi, Maria Sole, and that of the di Ferrero-Nasi. Regardless, while hard to trace and follow, the family still holds a significant fortune and many remain active in the management of that fortune.

Officially, the Agnelli family owns 53% of Exor through a separate holding company which takes its name from Fiat founder Giovanni Agnelli and pools dozens of his descendants as its investors.

Exor NV is a grand example, albeit, a little complicated. It's not really a family office, it is a large holding company that is primarily owned by the Agnelli family. Exor holds significant stakes in Ferrari, Juventus, and the CNH Industrial. The Agnelli family-controlled holding company has a market valuation of over $20B. At one time Exor held Perrier apart from countless other leading companies, all seemingly properly diversified.

Regardless, in 2015, in what was largely seen as a diversification move to separate interests with automobile and manufacturing, Exor NV bought PartnerRe, a Bermuda-based reinsurer for $6.5B. The investment was very successful and paid many dividends, totaling just over $650M in dividend payments since the purchase. In February of 2020 Covea, the French insurer, approached Exor to discuss talks to purchase PartnerRe for $9B, all cash. The deal ultimately fell through, but this example is nothing short of a fabulous example of an international family with multinational economic interest and hundreds of living descendants, remaining active in economic affairs and continuing to create value.

Bibliography

See Duchy of Lancaster official documents and history.
The Pictet Model, Witten Institute for Family Business, May 2017.

4

The Americas

No matter the location families operate businesses, own enterprises by default influence industry. If one is able to hold onto ownership and continue, generally the next step is to consolidate the organization of the enterprises within a hierarchy of sorts.

Apart from the private riches of royal families; extended royal cadet branches and aristocrats with state ties, the merchant class drove the development of household wealth in the merchant class. Merchants not only perpetuated their wealth and business lines through family connections, but were pioneers of international trade and technically created the first multinational partnerships. When the first multinational corporations began setting up new colonies, governors were appointed and with the responsibilities of state came the boom of population. These appointments were for the male of the family but generally benefited the entire family. One can make an educated assumption that first family offices were unknowingly interwoven within the state's affairs—or controlled the state's affairs. The collective management of family businesses and executive family offices have played important roles in the vassals of industry and commerce since the days of trade began.

C. Hagan, *Global Family Office Investing*,
https://doi.org/10.1007/978-3-030-18224-3_4

North America: From a Family Business to a Single Family Office

At this moment we are in the golden age of family offices, at least in America. While family office structures can clearly be attributed to the European practice of managing family assets and providing for households of royals and families of prominence the American market owns the modern space.

A family office is simply the executive management of permanent capital and assets. It is a natural progression of success and has been a tool of the upper class for estate planning and wealth management for a variety of reasons, the main being preservation of capital. Over the decades this active form of permanent capital management has become very popular and profitable, but its roots are steeped in centuries of economic history. In the modern age, with the surge in entrepreneurial activity, it is no surprise that first-generation millionaires and billionaires are electing to control and manage their permanent capital. In an era of new wealth and changing ways, if you take the ethos of a bulge bracket bank and how they view family offices, the most agile and capable of banks pivoted years back to better attract family offices and families of significant influence. It was clear early on that this new wave of family offices promised consistent revenues, long-term outlooks, and the ability to cater to a family through their entire wealth lifecycle.

In the traditional sense a family office is that of a management company for a single family utilizing a single family office structure (SFO) or that of a management company for multiple families inside a multifamily office (MFO). MFOs are largely wealth management tools when compared to an SFO. Typically a single family office is formed for the benefit of one family. By nature families evolve, so even the most permanent of institutions will vanish if they do not evolve. SFOs have similarities in that most handle one family—or the descendants of a one family. A single family office is created by one family and serves that family, even though their are other families that enter the picture from marriage and lifestyles. An heir is an heir despite the surname. More than often modern SFOs are formed from wealth created by a family business or an inheritance. SFOs handle family matters from family financial matters to major business decisions, asset management decisions and also planning and successions.

Most SFOs have a succession plan intact, and a commonality in SFOs is a solid conception of the succession plan with family members involved in the process of succession. One of the best modern examples is Room 5600, the fabled Rockefeller family office which supervised the five brothers fortunes received from John D. Rockefeller's only son John D. Rockefeller, Jr. Located at Rockefeller Center on the 56th floor in midtown Manhattan, the fortune was managed here for decades. Founded in 1882 the office has evolved and progressed to the point where it has lent the family name to a new MFO, Rockefeller Capital and downsized the original SFO located on the 56th floor to the smaller 1 Rockefeller Place. Perhaps not so ironic, in private practice I have found that a number of family's run family offices from the terrace levels—or basements—of commercial buildings they own.

Multifamily Office (MFO)

While similar to an SFO, MFOs differ in their arrangements. Generally structured as commercial concerns within banks or financial companies, MFOs tend to pool their resources for enhanced profitability while simultaneously increasing their customer service and customer experience to the clients to differentiate from competition such as a typical private bank or private wealth manager. It is worth noting that many MFOs operate as small RIAs that oversee a select number of families and that RIA is either an independent enterprise, a subsidiary of a bank or a separate company with preferred affiliation.

While the structure and concept of a family office has been around since the management of enterprise and economic concerns began, the growth of family offices in the past decade has been enormous. As mentioned, modern family offices are largely grouped in two prominent forms: the single family office (SFO) which revolves around a family and their respective business, associated enterprises, extended concerns, and wealth. A single family office may represent a growing family under one parental group or set of great-great-grandparents. The second is the more diverse multifamily office (MFO). This can simply be an oversized single family office that has grown accustomed to the needs of multiple families, or it can be a grouping of tech billionaires, a grouping of family millionaires or even a group of friends who worked together and made millions. Many times an MFO is created to house an expanding fortune to best group together a few hundred family members, many of whom may not associate with each other or even work together, the only commonality is they are distant cousins and shareholders. All of these scenarios are prevalent examples of modern SFOs and MFOs. A multifamily office means many things. As I have discussed throughout this book MFOs are varied in nature, just like the family office world. All of these scenarios are prevalent examples of modern MFOs. MFOs differ in size as some only foster very large fortunes and others take investors with net worth of $20M.

By combining multiple families less than one office there are savings to be found, services are combined, and at times the MFO can act like a bank, complete with branches across the country and immediate access to complex cash instruments for large purchases.

Multifamily offices mean quite a few things, just like SFOs, but the main difference is a commercialized system, or a CMFO. From a state level you have RIAs. RIAs are Registered Investment Advisors. This is common for a type of MFO as independent MFOs are dealing with a wide pool of people and multiple families, and likely advise individuals outside the exemptions. However, what are the differences between an MFO who advises wealthy families and an MFO which advises HNW and UHNW families? It is important to note that RIAs are also fiduciaries, which is terribly important in this day and age. Family offices should only work with ethical fiduciaries.

In my opinion the best MFO is within a private bank or a bank. MFO departments in banks have flexibility within services much higher margins than private banks, since they should offer capital markets and securities services in addition to money services and concierge services. Moreover, since fiduciary responsibility to the client is paramount it is also a marketing tool, and both the newly wealthy and those who have very old money should be steer clear of any category of money management and services that do not adhere to strict fiduciary and ethical laws.

The MFO Rockefeller Capital Management L.P. is located front and center of Rockefeller Center in Manhattan, now presenting and physically occupying a largess that the Rockefeller SFO used to project. They are also taking on a large group of MFOs within banks, or storied trust companies including but not limited to: Bessemer Trust, Northern Trust, Ayco (Goldman Sachs), Pictet, HSBC Private Bank, U.S. Trust, and CIBC to name a few. Bessemer and Northern are perhaps very well-known in America for family office services and private banking. A Northern Trust adviser could suggest to the family they establish a series of holding companies and LLCs, and create a voting structure, thereby establishing the beginning of a family office inside a bank servicing other family offices.

Not to be confused with a family office, investment clubs are very plentiful and they often tout shared risk and shared due diligence, but they can also perpetuate fear of missing out (FOMO). A family office should not suffer from FOMO. This is often joked about in the world of venture capital investing. VC and PE and Angel investing are all different but you generally have access to such inside an investment club. Clubs are useful if investors have limited direct investment experience; wish to join a group of like-minded investors or form an MFO. All clubs can be expected to differ and some will be highly capable with sophisticated investment pedigrees, others will utilize the membership to help on due diligence and strategy. As can be expected there are many clubs one can join from the very exclusive to smaller but vibrant angel investors. I personally know of a few that are quite worthwhile, from Atlanta to Long Island to Miami, and while I am not affiliated with them I do think this is a worthwhile approach for a family office that wants to network or perhaps demystify investing; they are even helpful if a family is looking to form a single family office. Many of these families and family offices have unique perspectives on their respective industries and regions as well as a concentrated system of asset control, often being able to move quickly if they need to make a core investment. Additionally, the brain trust that can be found is worth the relationship—this can help as a transitional education period while expanding or bringing new stakeholders to the industry. Above all clubs can be welcoming and that is important. Clubs are also building in stature and in the right geographic location a club could wield billions and billions dollars' worth of investment power.

Planning and Structure

Another way to look at a family office is to plan an inversion, that is a restructuring or expansion into a more efficient tax jurisdiction. This is almost always a cost savings move and families can set up individual companies for each beneficiary or incorporate a foundation and hold regular meetings on the islands. It greatly helps if a family member is willing to relocate to a tax-free jurisdiction for the benefit of the family, however, that is only necessary if a family member wishes to relocate as there are countless skilled professional adept at trust formation and management. North America has access to the best offshore zone in the world, particularly Bermuda, the Caymans, and the Bahamas.

To be forthright the employment force of a single family office greatly differs from that of a multifamily office. There are vastly different needs that need to be met by teams of specialists as well as executives who are skilled in sophisticated finance. For instance as far as the management of a multifamily office is concerned, one would need: private (or confidential) office assistants, analysts for the investment team, research assistants for the analysts, traders, and/or capital markets professionals to liaison with the trading desk and for trading needs of clients. Perhaps they need an aircraft leasing specialist (many times when people say they are buying a plane they enter into a lease agreement) or perhaps they need a team of personal assistants and concierge-type employees to provide a high touch level of service to demanding families.

On the flip side a single family office needs legal counsel, fiduciary finance professionals, and confidential assistants, as well as relationships with the best banks in the country. A model we used at Hagan Capital Group is to go to the source and that means banks involved as primary dealers of government debt. We do this because it serves us better in America, not necessarily in a global capacity. If you are in need of a global banking operation in America, again New York City is ideal because of the concentration of operations. In America it is acceptable to use regional banks for general cash management and business accounts; one should not risk capital markets and cash management on lower level talent. I will argue against using small regional banks for much other than a few accounts or sweep accounts.

In general family office employment resembles the management and asset management businesses. There are very long levels of retention. Executive management inside SFOs and MFOs vary, but with some regularity and SFO is more likely to have family members as a senior executive. MFOs at times remove family members from management completely by design, as do family-owned companies. At times family members are limited to take part in the management, other times family members are the real power. Staff from SFOs and MFOs have been known to leave and start their own family offices or funds, often with seed funding from their previous employer. It is a chummy world. This is a well-known observation in cities and regions with very powerful family-owned businesses and associated family foundations. Family offices are at the very least asset management firms and administration firms. Incomes for professionals in these fields are typical of their geographic competition and it is not unusual to find profit-sharing incentives among the very large and very wealthy family offices, be it SFO or MFO. SFOs tend to have smaller budgets and therefore tend to offer more conservative pay. In family offices where the business is financial trading, many of the executives receive an annual bonus commensurate with Wall Street bonuses.

Enter to more modern times, if we are to look at the family office of George Soros and how he plans, Mr. Soros can give away most of his estate and still remain one of the richest men on earth. Before transitioning from a hedge fund to a single family office Soros Fund Management, LLC had close to forty years of 20% annualized returns.[1] George found fame and fortune after forming an offshore fund called First Eagle Fund. First Eagle was one of the industries' early offshore hedge funds, and it was capitalized by the Arnold family who once employed George at the family investment bank of Arnhold and S. Bleichroeder. The level of success achieved by Soros

[1]Ahmed, Azam. "Soros to Close His Fund to Outsiders". DealBook. *New York Times*. Retrieved 26 September 2011.

created one of the world's greatest fortunes but it has been said he has a very small staff at his office. He also has complex philanthropic entities and has given away billions through his Open Society Foundations. The foundations fund organizations fighting for various freedoms, for transparent government accountability, and for equality all over the world. He even founded the Central European University. One can only guess that working for the Soros family office and foundation network is vastly different than working in other family offices and family foundations.

Regulation

The SEC has laid down a simple framework for what is a family office and how they are exempted from the RIA laws. Apart from securities laws and SEC federal and state RIA laws family offices have very few compliance issues unless they issue securities or take on unrelated and unemployed clients. Family offices are generally allowed to take employees' money for investment; however, this isn't a blanket state law. In fact it is safe to say that most states lack certain state laws pertaining to financial family offices outside RIA assets under management (AUM) regulations and the odd lot family limited partnership, family trust partnership, and collective family entity schemes.

As stated from the Securities and Exchange Commission regarding the Advisers Act of 1940:

> The Securities and Exchange Commission (the "Commission" or "SEC") regulates investment advisers, primarily under the Investment Advisers Act of 1940 (the "Advisers Act"), and the rules adopted under that statute (the "rules"). One of the central elements of the regulatory program is the requirement that a person or firm meeting the definition of "investment adviser" under the Advisers Act register with the Commission, unless exempt or prohibited from registration. Generally only larger advisers that have $25 million or more of assets under management or that provide advice to investment company clients are permitted to register with the Commission. Smaller advisers register under state law with state securities authorities. This document provides an overview of federal regulation, as applied to SEC-registered advisers. Many of the concepts discussed, however, also are relevant with respect to state-registered advisers.

Furthermore, a statement by Chairman Mary Schapiro U.S. Securities and Exchange Commission Washington, D.C. June 22, 2011 on family offices exempted the firms from registration:

> Next, we will consider adopting a new rule regarding the definition of "family office." In particular, the rule would enable those managing their own family's financial portfolios to determine whether their "family offices" can continue to be excluded from the Investment Advisers Act. Family offices are entities established by wealthy families to manage their money and provide tax and estate planning and similar services. Historically, such family offices have not been required to register with the SEC under the Advisers Act because of an exemption provided to investment advisers with fewer than 15 clients.

In the past family offices had avoided regulation by working with family members within ten generations of relation, or lineage; taking on less than 15 nonfamily clients per year, as well as not advertising. Though Dodd–Frank[2] had a grandfather clause, the regulation exempting family offices from registration had quite a ripple effect.

The SEC Family Office Ruling

> On June 22, 2011 the Commission adopted rule 202(a)(11)(G)-1 that defines "family offices" to be excluded from regulation under the Investment Advisers Act of 1940. "Family offices" are entities established by wealthy families to manage their wealth and provide other services to family members, such as tax and estate planning services.
>
> Family offices that are excluded from Advisers Act under the rule.
>
> Provides investment advice about securities only to "family clients," as defined by the rule;
>
> Is wholly owned by "family clients" and is exclusively controlled by "family members" and/or "family entities," as defined by the rule; and
>
> Does not hold itself out to the public as an investment adviser.
>
> Permissible family clients.
>
> Family members. Family members include all lineal descendants (including by adoption, stepchildren, foster children, and, in some cases, by legal guardianship) of a common ancestor.

---

[2]The Dodd–Frank Wall Street Reform and Consumer Protection Act that was enacted on July 21, 2010.

Key employees. Key employees include:

Executive officers, directors, trustees, general partners, or persons serving in a similar capacity for the family office or its affiliated family office; and

Other family clients. Other family clients generally include:

Any non-profit or charitable organization funded exclusively by family clients;

Any estate of a family member, former family member, key employee, or subject to certain conditions, a former key employee;

Certain family client trusts; and

Any company wholly-owned by, and operated for the sole benefit of, family clients[3]" (Figs. 4.1, and 4.2).

Planning for the Future

Family offices in North America are closely associated with family-controlled private foundations, family foundations and charitable trusts. These foundations serve many purposes from basic estate planning and tax-efficient planning to actual philanthropic gifting and multiple generational aspirations. It is common for foundations to hold the majority of cash reserves and assets.

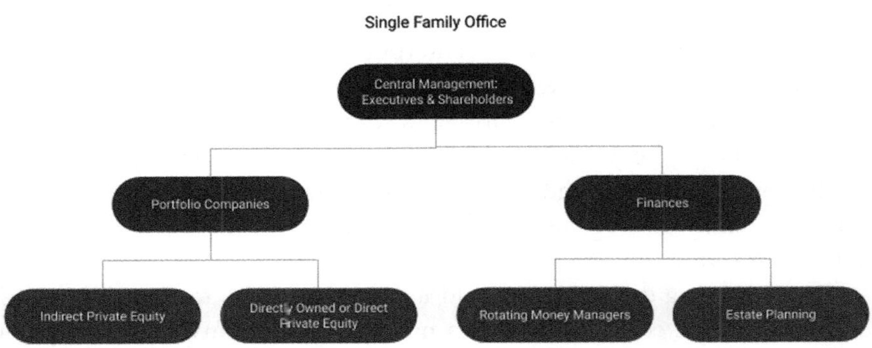

Fig. 4.1 Types of family offices

[3]SEC Family Office Ruling. June 22, 2011.

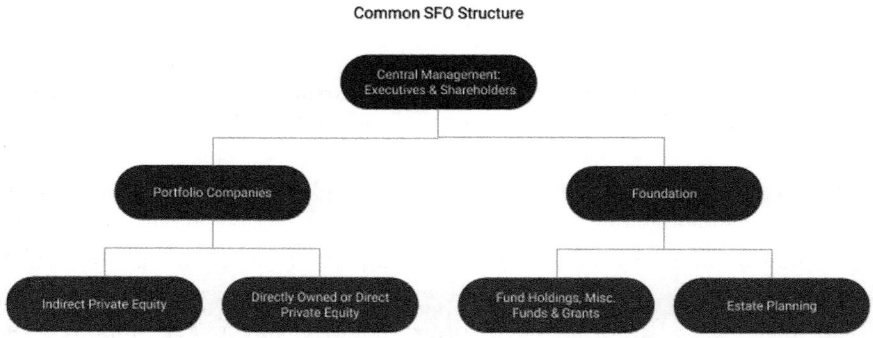

Fig. 4.2 Common SFO structures in America

There is no right way to disperse an estate in America or North America at large. What we have are customs and cultural norms but even those have been outpaced by modernity and family history. In America state law can come in effect but overall because of the higher income nature of family offices expenditures such as multimillion dollar life insurance are readily affordable are invested into life insurance to offset any estate taxes or often to create income for new trusts for descendants.

Inside a tightly held private company the rules are different than those of a public company. Private industry is much different than public entities, and a large majority of private companies are owned by families. This is clear and evident in many ways but the most prevalent in ownership. In private entities often decisions are weighted to executives or the most senior for whatever reason, so while changes may seem democratic they are in fact at times drastic. Family offices are no different.

Family members are as likely to work inside the family enterprise as they are to not work within the family enterprise. In North America established family offices are as likely to have family members and nonfamily members dominate the ranks of the enterprise and some are completely void of family work influence. The situations largely depend on the family at hand. It is common for siblings and offsprings to grow up in the family business or in the family management office and be comfortable working in that environment for a long-term career.

There is often a diverse sense of ideas when families are planning and the complications are compounded with multiple generations, and perhaps one important element to remember is that history and legacies can last forever but it is unlikely that a family office will last forever. However, it is possible for the family office to create other family offices for descendants, while cohesively investing the fortune in a way to create for scores of generations. In all sincerity it truly depends on the goals of the family and the family office creator(s).

Despite the perils and often accompany family enterprises family offices can establish a governing basis, laws and account for funding for many generations to come. Such happens frequently in North American family businesses and there are brilliant examples in the firms C.F. Martin & Co. (1833) which makes Martin guitars and the construction company Gilbane (founded 1873). The US-based C. F. Martin & Co has remained in family hands for six generations and today is run by Chairman and CEO Christian Frederick Martin IV.

In America family office succession differs greatly from enterprise to enterprise, but is not unlike private companies. Family members are not automatically assured positions in the enterprise however they are often shareholders of the family enterprise. Such dichotomies exist fluidly especially when multigenerational family management is intertwined. One can generally expect the two predominant forms of leadership; leadership in the form of management and ownership, and leadership in the form of voting share, and seniority.

Bechtel (1898) has been led by the Bechtel family since day one. Bechtel is a very significant firm in San Francisco and also the DC area (it is headquartered in Reston, Virginia). Led by the great-great-grandson of the founder is also the quintessential family business: Bechtel has been led, with a brief exception, by a succession of four family CEOs since cattle farmer Warren Bechtel founded the firm in 1898 to help build railroad lines. Bechtel is over 100 years old. A short list of projects includes a notable amount of global landmarks: the Hoover Dam; the Trans-Arabian Pipeline; the Bay Area Rapid Transit (BART), NASA's Space Launch Complex; the Channel Tunnel; Athens Metro (2004); and more recently engineered extensions to the London Underground.

Bechtel is an exemplary example of a family-held and family-managed enterprise. Few enterprises are as cohesive and have such longevity in the marketplace.

Trusts are quite popular in common law countries but they are not bulletproof nor are trusts and trustees always focused on conserving capital for future generations. With these points it is easy to see how trust assets evaporate

Age, health, marital status, and needs of the beneficiaries

- The grantor's intention and purpose for the trust.
- How each beneficiary is to be treated regarding their priority for distributions.
- The length of time the trust is intended to last.
- Anticipated current and future beneficiary distributions.

– Tax and estate planning consequences Illiquid or non-incoming producing assets in the trust.

Family Feuds

Families do not have to like each other or even love each other but it is helpful to the finances if they elect to stick together. It is best practice to put aside the usual personal egos that accompany generational entrepreneurship or entitlement for the integrity of the family holdings, as preservation of capital and the integrity of finances for future generations are often the main concern. However, entrepreneurship and do-it-yourself attitudes lead to families deciding to break up holdings and liquidate, thereby diminishing the family holdings and diluting the assets at hand, not factoring in last minute sales or other issues. Families are as likely to get along as they are to disagree. Communication and mutual respect is the backbone of healthy familial relationships, but that is easier said than done and oversized fortunes often create oversized issues. This is very common; perhaps the commonality among family offices is the propensity to disagree. I am asked this question all the time and I have seen fractures in families of all types, and with generational change it is almost guaranteed. After all families evolve through life and death; they do not clamber together and move down the family tree in a huddled mass. The best practice in this scenario is to make do for any stakeholders who have serious irreversible issues—often it can mean buying out the family members' shares if disagreements percolate into operations. Granted situations have to be made for future generations of that branch—so the negotiations are high stakes and attention to details for equitable treatment is ideal. In a family office situation shooting for a century plus of management you cannot be sidelined by generational disagreement. Additionally, it is often within reach for family offices to establish managed offices or trusts for decedents and family members who may suffer temporary or permanent setbacks.

Complete buyouts are not uncommon, nor is a retooling of the assets and reorganization of the finances and shareholders every few years. Succession is perhaps the most important event in a family enterprise, as every person retires and expires. Often we see powerful people holding onto power for as long as they can, grappling with their own mortality among their final dwindling days. This is to be expected in some circumstance and as long as the plan protects and provides for future generations, succession is what binds

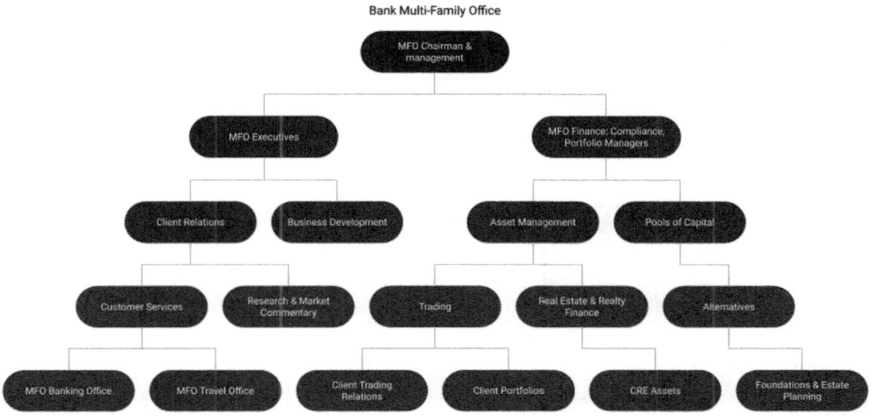

Fig. 4.3 Bank MFO family office structure

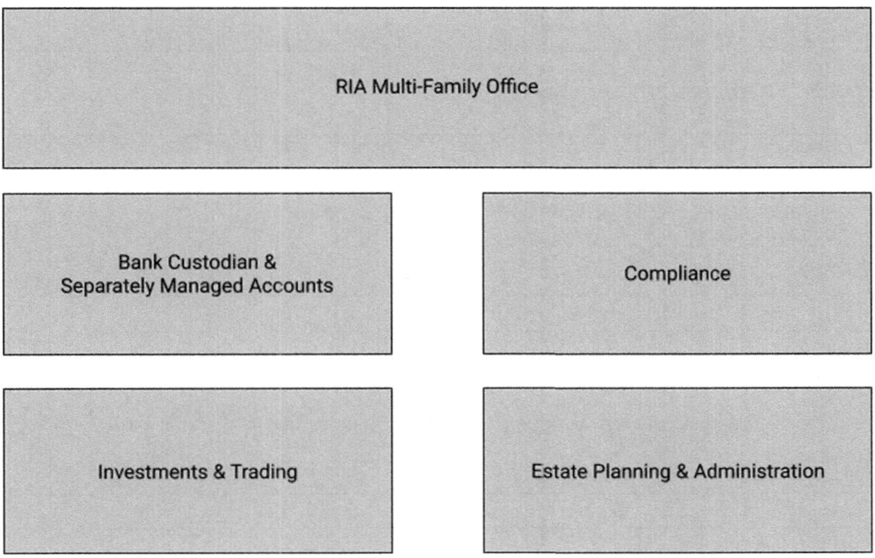

Fig. 4.4 RIA MFO structure example

the fortune, trust, or foundation together for as long as one can maintain it (Figs. 4.3, 4.4, 4.5, and4.6).

American Legacies

More and more international families view the United States as a safe haven. The multitude of states and competitive state laws and the robust US domestic market continue to attract attention. The United States is seen as

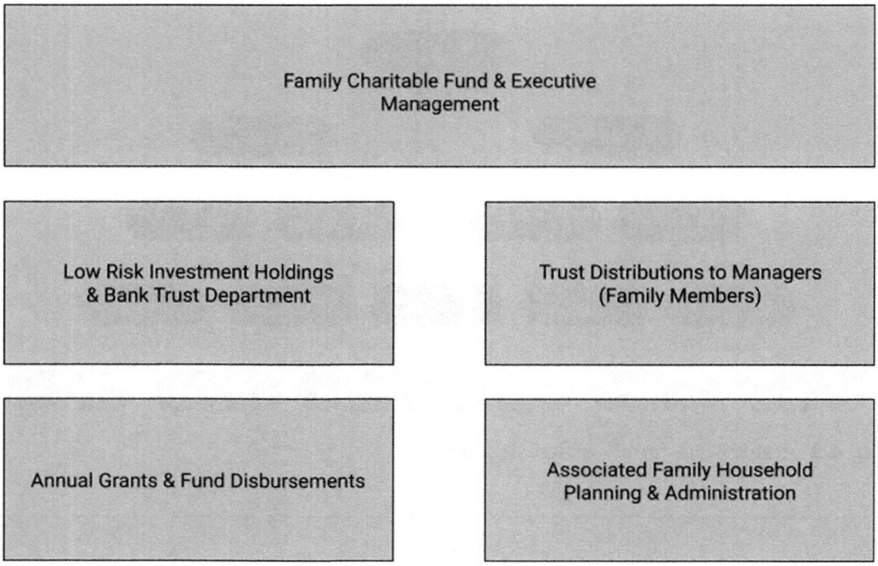

Fig. 4.5 Charitable fund example

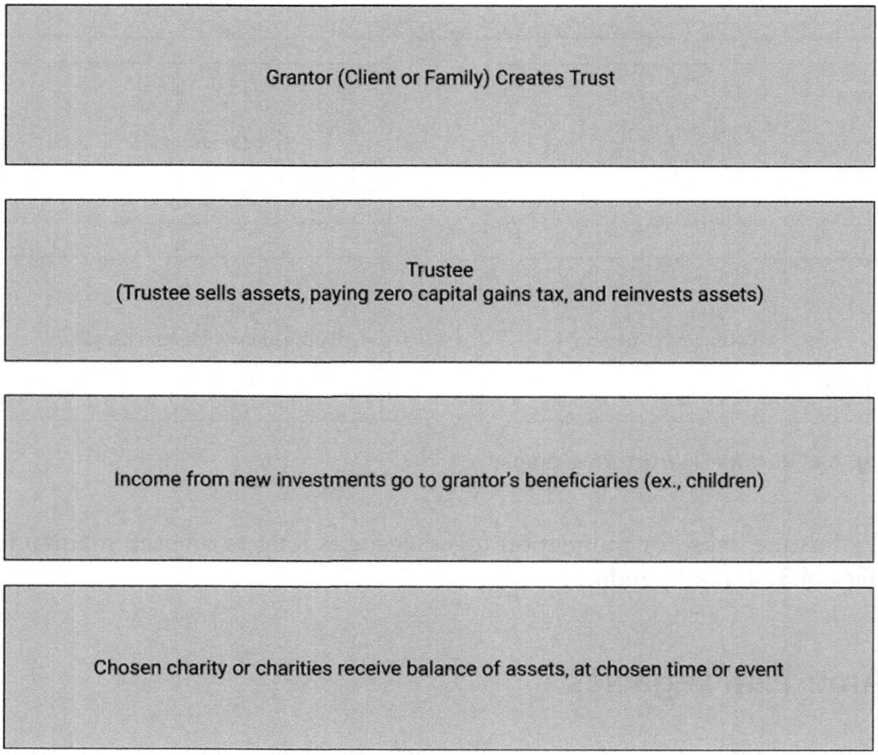

Fig. 4.6 Charitable remainder trust example

a nation where you can build generational wealth if you play your cards—or invest your money—strategically. Ironically, many wealthy families will never see their family fortunes grow past the third generation. This is often referred to as the 3rd generation rule. There is a Chinese saying: 富不过三代 or fu bu guo san dai; which when translated means "wealth does not pass three generations." There is no simple explanation as to why wealth is spent in such a short time, but a large majority of such scenarios can be blamed on mismanagement, negligence, and lack of communication.

In America the legend of self-made men exists to such an extent that successful entrepreneurs and businessmen who hail from prosperous, millionaire families often refer to themselves as self-made despite receiving incredible wealth and opportunity by birth alone. In fact it is seen as almost un-American by the middle class and meritocracy classes to expect full inheritances and to live on inherited money without having gainful employment. This contradiction has led to an informal "half-inheritance half-opportunity system" for many upper middle and upper classes of America. Because of this it is my opinion through observation that the American way has led to a degree of "negligible management" toward succession, estate planning, and wealth management inside America's wealthy classes. Perhaps magical thinking has allowed for an inflated reliance on the "half-inheritance half-opportunity system" in America and this promise of easy money to compliment a modest inheritance has eroded the belief of steadfast and prudent management of financials.

Another side to this spectrum is the Carnegie and Rockefeller family. Carnegie literally gave most all of his wealth away, to the point that current descendants are not noted for their inherited Carnegie billions. The Carnegie legacy lives on, not only through the Carnegie Corporation but also socially. Skibo Castle in Scotland, Carnegie's former Scottish home is now managed by the Carnegie Club. By comparison some Rockefeller heirs are still billionaires.

Case Study - Room 5600

> John D. Rockefeller's family office, Rockefeller & Co., was founded in 1882. It began selling its expertise to other families in 1980, and by mid-2008 it had $28 billion of clients' assets under its hood.
>
> —Richard C. Morais, Barrons, September 15, 2012

John D. Rockefeller was born on July 8, 1839, in Richford, New York. In 1870 he formed the Standard Oil Company. By June 1891 John D. was reported to be the wealthiest American, with about $150,000,000 and an income of $25,000 per day.

In the 1880s, John D. Rockefeller formed Rockefeller & Co. to manage his growing fortune. For nearly 100 years the Rockefeller family office enjoyed a good amount of privacy up until the nomination of Nelson Rockefeller for vice president of America. After President Richard Nixon resigned Gerald Ford became president and he nominated Nelson Rockefeller to be the VP. A robust investigation of the family finances ensued.

Entitled "probing The Rockefeller Fortune" the probe takes one inside "Room 5600" which was long headquartered at New York's Rockefeller Center. The report found a number of interlinking interests of ownership and the use of dozens and dozens (if not hundreds) of trusts. Room 5600, which was the nexus of Rock & Co. and occupied a floor at Rockefeller Center, which at one time employed over 200 people to manage the families individual accounts. Significant reporting was done to highlight the involvement of the Rockefeller families international investments and development, as well as trusts, single family member accounts, and philanthropy.

In the 1980s Rockefeller & Co. debuted Rockefeller Financial Services, which was designed to manage money for other wealthy families. Later, in the late 1990s, the family debuted Rockit Command, an IT platform.

In 2012 the family sold a 37% stake to Lord Jacob Rothschild's RIT Capital Partners, RIT bought the interest from Société Générale Private Banking. Rockefeller Financial Services works for the Rockefellers, rather than the other way round. However, family members sit on the board, and they remain influential.

In 2014 the family downsized and moved from their three-story suite of offices and floors and moved to 1 Rockefeller Plaza. The next commercial phase of the family is Rockefeller Capital, a high-flying multifamily office and trust company with offices in most major markets, bespotted with celebrity board members and Rockefeller family members as advisors.

Central American and the Caribbean

In 2016 an offshore scandal soon labeled "The Panama Papers" emerged. As the scandal unraveled details showed an operation of epic proportions. Celebrities and political leaders were implicated, with over 200,000 entities exposed all from the records of one law firm based in Panama City, Panama, Central America. In due time the firm came under intense scrutiny and would ultimately shutter, maintaining innocence to this day.

While economic hubs in Central America are busy developing just across the Caribbean you will find the most establish offshore players in the business. From the British Virgin Islands and Caymans Island to the Bahamas and ultimately Bermuda, these offshore hubs in the British Overseas Territories see more fund management, trust, and family office business than you could ever imagine. In 2018 the Institute on Taxation and Economic Policy (ITEP) estimated $2.6 trillion was offshore, and while it is hard to track the flow of international currency, offshore centers are the de facto clearing houses for offshore activity.

Most will attest to not knowing of any dodgy practices in the British Overseas offshore zones. Many have grown accustomed to international corporates and families using offshore zones for custody of assets and jurisdictions of funds, but it could also be that the newer market participants in Central America are pushing the envelope to see just how far they can take it.

South America

Countries in South America view the United States as the ultimate offshore zone, safe from whatever dictators or feeble regime is in power. South America is filled with colonial history, vast natural resources, and some of the most troubled economies and governments in the world. While this is not without attempts, South America and its economies remain a mixed bag of mercantilist policies favoring domestic economies with intense overlays of corruption. Venezuela is a noted example of corruption but nearly all South American countries have seen their fair share of scandals in the modern era. At best this large swath of area is still finding its footing, individually, but inequality has a great stronghold.

International bankers tend to perk up anytime they hear about a growing middle class, as it is time for consumer loans to fund materialistic dreams, but when South America is booming in this modern era you can bet it is doing so at someone else's expense. Peru, Ecuador, Brazil, Colombia, Chile, Bolivia, Venezuela, all cluster together, separated by the Andes, the Andean plateau the Amazon basin; to the north you have the Caribbean, Central America with the Panama Canal; to the south you have a tip that reaches Antarctica; a wildly different set of countries with a booming set of economies intertwined with America and the rest of the developed world until the Great Depression. The commodity curse withstanding, South America is international in a way only compared to Europe, due to natural borders among a smattering of countries; yet they have a long history of paying attention only to domestic issues. However, despite perceived negatives the continents have ample room for economic growth and over the last decades we have seen household wealth in Brazil explode (Fig. 4.7).

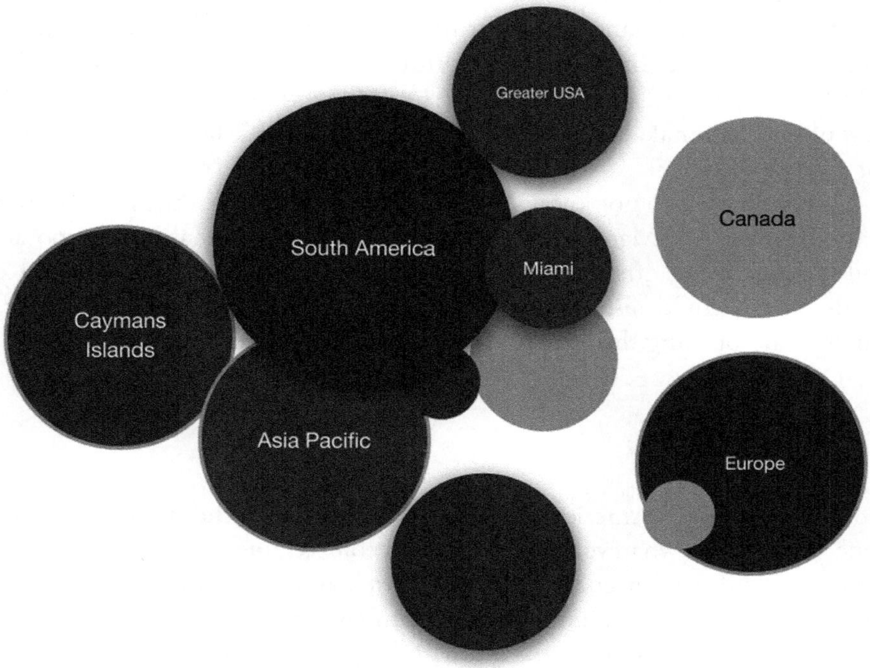

Fig. 4.7 South America second branch

Overview and Structures

Since 1930 the countries of South America collectively have practiced import substitution industrialization (ISI), a trade mechanism and policy that put domestic production ahead of foreign imports or imports at all. ISI above all is a trade and tariff tool like mercantilism and economic protectionism and the use of such policy encouraged domestic reinvestment and domestic stabilization from a state level.

ISI is rooted in the PSH theory—the Prebisch–Singer Hypothesis—which states that commodity prices decline over time when compared to manufactured goods. This realization hit commodity countries hard because of which they adapted a unique mercantilism perspective for their economies. In his

World Bank paper: A New Structural Economics, Justin Yifu Lin explains in great detail the structural issues that plagued South America:

> The slump of international trade in the Great Depression led to export pessimism in the Post-War period. In Latin America for instance, political leaders and social élites were influenced strongly by the deterioration in the terms of trade, the economic difficulty encountered during the Great Depression in the 1930s and the thesis developed by Prebisch (1950) and Singer (1950). They argued that the way for a developing country to avoid being exploited by developed countries was to develop domestic manufacturing industries through a process known as import substitution. Moreover, the emergence of previous colonies or semi-colonies as newly independent states in Asia and the Middle East, and later in Africa, was accompanied by strong nationalist sentiments. Compared with developed countries, these developing countries had an extremely low economic growth rate and per capita gross national product, high birth and death rates, low average educational attainments and very backward infrastructure. They were heavily specialized in the production and export of primary commodities and imported most of their manufactured goods. Thus, it was central to every developing government's national agenda to develop its economy independently so as to achieve a rapid economic take-off and eliminate poverty. The Latin American debt crisis began in 1982 when international financial markets realized that some countries, which had unlimited access to foreign capital after the collapse of the Bretton Woods system, were not able to pay back their loans.[4]

It is safe to say that North and South America were in a sort of blissful economic union with deep trading agreements and economic integration before the American Great Depression struck. Once the depression stuck and austerity sank in, interest in international trade waned. The economic union was short lived, and further integration scaled back and grinded to a halt, with most South American countries diving deep into their respective ISI policies.

The Prebisch–Singer hypothesis served as the basis for the dependency theory which argued that wealthier countries had an unfair advantage over poorer countries in relation to trade; raw commodity prices compared to the prices of finished manufactured goods from America did not equal out, in fact prices were diminishing more and more over time. This developed into the structuralist school of thought which reflected on the dynamics stemming from global economic structures and their relation to local economics with unique characteristics.

[4]New Structural Economics: A Framework for Rethinking Development. World Bank Group.

Harrods, the upmarket department store, opened its only location outside of the London area in Buenos Aires. It was opened in 1914 and lasted until the end of the century. Argentina has a rich history that dissipated once economic stagnation became the norm in 1975. The British took to Argentina and helped develop a large agricultural sector that would only be replaced by Brazil. Argentina was an economic leader in the nineteenth century. After independence in 1810 Argentina leapt to the challenge with great entrepreneurship and international trade. When the great Depression hit Argentina had shielded most of the contagion by removing the gold standard in December of 1929. Despite the maestro move additional policies would lead Argentina into an extended spiral.

This is where the narrative against IMF and American intervention was initially formed when it in fact is the opposite. The ISI policy used by Latin American governments helped the countries avoid the plague of the Great Recession. By 1975 the growth was gone. From 1975 until 1990 Argentina entered a period of pronounced stagnation, a period of austerity, tremendous economic loss, and unfathomable inflation. Argentina reached out to the IMF in 1982, the first of many bailouts and scandals. Argentina suffered more setbacks in the early 2000s, before a renewed period of positive outlook walking into the administration of President Macri. This renewed hope dissipated as Argentina again descended into economic chaos. Argentina's period of pronounced stagnations and corruption is linked to many different views, but perhaps the most prominent is the continued criticism of ISI policy and IMF credit programs, both of which still exist throughout South America.

Cargill, Bunge, and some of the more established family-owned commodity trading companies with investments and operations in South America have subsidiaries in the Caymans to handle the movement of assets. I can only imagine smaller players follow the same path. When the US tariffs halted soybeans exports a large purchase of US soybeans from Argentina came in. Later it was shown that Argentina fulfilled the orders to a degree for China to meet state soy demands. It is true that the United States at large is a recipient of such fortunes and fees from South America, especially when compared to other developed and rich countries the United States is often the safest apart from Canada. The point is to capture fluid business on this hemisphere, despite the political woes on the continents. Any group with a history of trading any trade in South America is very accustomed to outlandish political turmoil.

Brazil's famous billionaire, Jorge Paulo Lemann, founded Banco Garantia in 1971. It was said he envisioned Banco Garantia as Brazil's Goldman Sachs, and in many ways he was right. Lemann is now one of the world's richest men, and he has teamed up with more of the world's richest including Warren Buffet and Continental Grain Company for some of the world largest takeovers and direct investments. His homeland, Brazil, eclipses the rest of South America by virtue of GDP alone and market capitalization, but not when you divide the GDP with Brazil's population. Brazil still relies on ISI to support domestic growth, and can be described as a mixed economy working through a culture of graft. Brazil, much like the rest of Latin and South America invests internally and for domestic revenues. This can be considered par for the course. Family businesses will reinvest in their businesses to ensure the promise of stability and then move funds offshore. One unique aspect to South American fortunes, family business-driven family offices and enterprising family offices is that they are quite used to working at an international level—for safety. Miami is often the receipt of such foreign capital. It is often said that Miami is the capital of Latin America. In a retrospective article from the Federal Reserve of Atlanta, staff writer Charles Davidson sheds light on Miami's intense international growth brought on by South American business and finance influence:

> The initial surge of Cuban exiles set in motion Miami's emergence as an international banking center. Political and economic events in Latin American and the Caribbean sparked significant capital flight into Miami beginning in the 1970s. As a result, many domestic and international banks offered wealth management services for foreign clients.[5]

This has only grown and now South Florida is a well-established international financial hub. If you remember the UBS tax dodging scandal that originated in South Florida, this was due to the high concentration of wealth, international interests, and financial company clustering, in addition to a history of private banking over the last fifty years. This has only increased. South Florida—and Miami in particular—has not only successfully attracted the businesses of New York's Wall Street but also businesses of California's Silicon Valley.

South America is not without domestic tax havens, and while outside of Miami one generally thinks toward Panama, Chile actually has attractive tax laws for foreign corporations and from this Chile attracts a healthy amount of Latin American and international business. Though still deeply rooted in commodity production, Santiago and surrounding areas have been noted for

[5]FBR Atlanta, Charles Davidson, "Miami: From Land Rushes to Massive Immigration, December 20, 2018".

their progressive and liberal attitudes to business and expansion, including low tax and no tax on foreign corporates who trade in Chile:

> Chile has been one of Latin America's fastest-growing economies in recent decades, enabling the country to significantly reduce poverty. Between 2000 and 2015, the population living in poverty (on US$ 4 per day) decreased from 26 percent to 7.9 percent. Responsible macroeconomic and fiscal management provides a solid base for more inclusive growth. To achieve this potential, however, Chile needs to build consensus to respond to the expectations of a growing middle class at the same time it increases economic growth potential. In the short term, it is crucial to recover the trust of the private sector to stimulate investment in sectors in addition to mining. In the longer term, the country must address structural challenges to promote productivity, improve energy provision, and reduce dependence on mining and increase access to and quality of social services.[6]

Corporate Structures

I have included a listing of the most common forms of entity registration for family office systems and networks in Latin America. I have left out sole proprietary ownerships, branch offices, foundations, and foreign-registered corporation (foreign corporations) as associated costs and taxes outweigh those benefits, and from an international point of view unless one is domiciled with business interests there and never cares to leave, any family association would greatly benefit by using an unaffected country or territory like Bermuda, the Bahamas, the Caymans, the United States, or Canada.

Common types of Latin American entities:

Argentina:
Corporation: Sociedad Anónima (S.A.)
Simplified Shares Company: Sociedad por Acciones Simplificadas (S.A.S)
Limited Liability Company: Sociedad de Responsabilidad Limitada (LTDA, SRL)
Brazil:
Limited Liability Companies ("Limitadas" or "Ltda.")
Limited Liability Corporation (S/A)
Silent Partnership (SCPs)
Colombia:

[6]World Bank, September 24, 2018.

Simplified stock companies (SAS)
Limited liability companies (LTDA)
Corporations (SA)

Chile:
General partnership (Sociedad Colectiva)
Share company (Sociedad por Acciones)
Limited liability partnership (Sociedad de Responsabilidad Limitada)
Association (Associación, or Cuentas en Participación)

Uruguay:
Corporation (Sociedad Anónima—S.A.)
General partnerships (Sociedades Colectivas)
Limited partnerships (Sociedades en Comandita)

The Business of Inheritance

There is a tremendous amount of corruption present throughout Latin America. One scandal eclipses another scandal in domestic and international media. The most recent scandal: Operation Car Wash is the largest corruption scandal Latin America has even seen. To date it has uprooted numerous elected officials in various South American countries and involves a plethora of South American firms, all guilty for bribery.

One of the offshore and commercial finance hubs of Latin American—apart from Miami—is Panama. Panama and the Panama Canal is an industrial hub of global trade, financial services, and tourism. Panama and finance have long had a shadowy history. It was long considered a trustee and funding haven for offshore North American money.

As for offshore trustee duties, Panama is clearly a front runner in this department as an established system of trustees and law firms hold a large chunk of trust and offshore estate administration and power of attorney privileges.

While the past few decades have seen new wealth created many of those have yet to plan accordingly and the market is just beginning to see such. Oddly it resembles Russia to a degree. Mass amount of wealth single handling appearing, disappearing and or lost. The regimes are otherworldly. Apart from flat-out crime you have lawlessness and inflation has been rampant it is not a deep aspect of South America's economic history. Guyana has one of the more stable inflation rate histories, and oil exploration and production investment is ticking up, but infrastructure investments are still in need, and with a developing population base it is hard to depend on purely tax revenues. Uruguay is viewed as a safe haven inside South America, but there has been a crackdown over such practices. Chile has favorable tax treatment and imposed zero tax on foreign corporations. Spanish culture dictates males adopted the last name of the mother, so it can be hard to follow the money. This makes one need to specialize in Spanish and Latin familiar practices.

It is very challenging to plan for the future in a set of economies where law can at times seem secondary and policy can seem more experimental. Uruguay long suffered infighting and civil wars, with almost constant fighting between 1830 and 1903, a historical characteristic shared by other South American countries. Today it is much different, and since 2004 Uruguay has achieved stable growth, year after year (for the most part), with a liberal agriculture export economy, low poverty, and legal marijuana.

> Uruguay rates high for most development indicators and is known for its secularism, liberal social laws, and well-developed social security, health, and educational systems. It is one of the few countries in Latin America and the Caribbean where the entire population has access to clean water. Uruguay's provision of free primary through university education has contributed to the country's high levels of literacy and educational attainment.[7]

Uruguay stands apart in Latin America for its high income per capita and low level of poverty. The middle class in Uruguay represents more than 60% of its population over 70% of the workforce is employed in professional services and over 90% of the population lives in the urban area of Montevideo.

Wealthy citizens in the country neighboring Uruguay often have accounts and holding company's domiciled in the country. Uruguay has a tradition of banking secrecy, cash handling, and custody. Much of this revolves around Uruguay's recent history as a stable stronghold with liberal economics, but that is a modern attribute. Client information at financial institutions is protected. Supervising entities enforce strict compliance, and constant communication is maintained with the BCU (Central Bank of Uruguay) sharing metrics on credit, but not client accounts unless there is a substantial reason.

These are the only times client information may be shared:

- By an interested party, issued in writing (such as Argentina's Tax office)
- By duly sustained resolution of the Courts (Court mandate)
- By BCU related to the organization, operations, and monitoring of financial institutions.

[7] *The World Factbook 2018*, Central Intelligence Agency.

- After 30 days of indicted by the tax authority for tax fraud
- By Court order, in conjunction with the Uruguay Director of the Tax Office (DGI), for domestic tax issues.

Today, Uruguay does share information with their neighbors but this was not the case for years. Many wealthy citizens in Brazil and Argentina had accounts in Uruguay that hold money from assets and business dealings done domestically, but conceal ownership through structures in Panama. The Panama Papers put an end to an era to a degree, but many of these structures are already in place. Additionally, since South America is still in constant economic flux, corruption and the mixing of illegal and legal activities will continue, coupled with jurisdiction stacking and offshore activity.

Case Study: Argentina and Wealth

Hedge fund manager Paul Singer spent 15 years battling the government of Argentina over a botched bond issuance. When it was all said and done his investment firm, Elliot Management and subsidiary NML Capital, took home more than four times the original investment, which had invested in Argentina sovereign bonds. At one point the Argentine government attempted to renegotiate and Singer refused to take a loss on his investment, taking further legal action against Argentina by detaining one of Argentina's naval training vessels (the ARA Libertad) when it docked in Tema, Ghana, on the Atlantic coast of Africa. President Cristina Fernandez was forced to charter aircrafts over fears that Argentina's version of Air Force One would be seized.

While unprecedented in modern times, this issue was eventually settled. Argentina filed that the action broke the Foreign Sovereign Immunities Act of 1976, while the "Second Circuit affirmed, rejecting Argentina's argument that the District Court's order transgressed the Foreign Sovereign Immunities Act of 1976 (FSIA or Act)…no provision in the FSIA immunizes a foreign-sovereign judgment debtor from post judgment discovery of information concerning its extraterritorial assets." Furthermore, the court affirmed: Argentina's arguments are unavailing. Even if Argentina were correct that §1609 execution immunity implies coextensive discovery in-aid-of-execution immunity, the latter would not shield from discovery a foreign sovereign's extraterritorial assets, since the text of §1609 immunizes only foreign-state property in the United States. The prospect that NML's general request for information about Argentina's worldwide assets may turn up information about property that Argentina regards as immune does not mean that NML cannot pursue discovery of it."[8]

I have illuminated the issue here because it involved the Republic of Argentina, a few hedge funds in New York, and ultimately the US courts, which I found quite exciting and original. It's not that often you hear of a country fighting off hedge funds from taking state assets.

I have found from my own professional experience that many South Americans and Argentines view America as an excellent country to establish a family office or a family-owned investment company. In my experience the US states of Texas, Florida, and California; the British Virgin Islands and the Cayman Islands—have attracted the most Argentine investment dollars and family office structures. Outside of the major metropolitan areas of New York City and Los Angeles, the majority of Argentina Americans reside in South Florida and Houston[9], per the 2010 US Census.

Bibliography

See "Soros to Close His Fund to Outsiders". *New York Times*. September 26, 2011.

See The Dodd–Frank Wall Street Reform and Consumer Protection Act, July 21, 2010.

SEC Family Office Ruling. June 22, 2011.

See New Structural Economics: A Framework for Rethinking Development. World Bank Group.

See Federal Reserve Bank of Charles Davidson, "Miami: From Land Rushes to Massive Immigration." December 20, 2018.

From the World Bank, September 24, 2018.

From the Central Intelligence Agency, *World Factbook 2018* edition.

From the court case, REPUBLIC OF ARGENTINA v. NML CAPITAL, LTD. THE UNITED STATES COURT OF APPEALS FOR THE SECOND CIRCUIT. Argued April 21, 2014–Decided June 16, 2014.

From the 2010 US Census.

[8]REPUBLIC OF ARGENTINA v. NML CAPITAL, LTD. THE UNITED STATES COURT OF APPEALS FOR THE SECOND CIRCUIT. Argued April 21, 2014–Decided June 16, 2014.

[9]2010 United States Census.

5

India and Asia Pacific

The Pacific Rim has become a multicity hub for FOs, from Singapore to Hong Kong to Taipei, Sydney, and Jakarta. Singapore has taken over large swaths of the commodity physical trade involving shipping, raw materials and consumer goods of all types; luring banks and financial companies to their port with the allure of safety and a world-class luxury lifestyle. China on the other hand is the bona fide home of the new ultrarich and super rich, with offshore Taipei, Taiwan, actually serving as the older money of sorts. Before Taiwan enjoyed offshore independence Taiwan was under Japanese rule and it is the Japanese that should be thanked for Taiwan's industrial prowess. This laid the foundation for modern day Taiwan. Unlike typical colonial powers Japan focused on developing Taiwan into a modern economy, introducing modern communications, railroads, banking systems, public health, and agriculture irrigation systems.[1] In 1945 Japan lost control of Taiwan and Taiwan fell under the control of the Republic of China (ROC), who permanently relocated to Taiwan in 1949. The ROC claims to be the legitimate China, though this is disputed by mainland China, which is ruled by the Communist Party of China (CPC), the only governing party of the People's Republic of China (PRC). Regardless, by the 1960s Taiwan was off to the races, free from the PRC and free to continue with the United States, who in turn helped the country develop into an industrial powerhouse.

[1] "The Four Little Dragons", Ezra F. Vogel. 1991.

C. Hagan, *Global Family Office Investing*,
https://doi.org/10.1007/978-3-030-18224-3_5

While some confusion may persist, Taiwan is a separate aspect of China, though mainland China disagrees. China took control of Taiwan in 1945, which had been formerly occupied by Japan since 1895. In 1949 Taiwan reverted to martial law and was led as a single-party state under the leader Chiang Kai-shek. Reforms came about in the 1980s, which then led to a presidential election in the mid-1990s. Today Taiwan very much views itself as a separate country from China—a republic country with the official name being the Republic of China (ROC)—while mainland China views Taiwan as a China-affiliated republic offshoot.

Despite there being two China's since 1949 (China which is in fact Taiwan, and ruled by the ROC and mainland China ruled by the PRC), mainland China has turned a blind eye to Taiwan, but over recent years they have gained control of Hong Kong, making it clear they are intent on playing by the mainland China rulebook. When the US Secretary of State Mike Pompeo remarked on radio on November 12, 2020 that Taiwan was not part of China there was immediate pushback by the Chinese. China went as far to say that US–Taiwan relations were a point of contention. In the near future I expect increasing tension regarding Taiwan's independent status, closely following the deterioration of Hong Kong's independence with mainland China. It seems as if China's PRC is solely focused on One China, meaning Hong Kong and Taiwan must embrace a hybrid model of republic and communist politics, along with a hybrid of market capitalism and China's state capitalism.

It is impossible to discuss Asia's major economies without discussing the concept of state capitalism or the East Asian Model. The East Asian Model of capitalism refers to state involvement and intervention in commerce and a high household rate of household savings and investments, high educational standards, and export-oriented policy. This is how China operates, for instance, a mixture of market-based goals with heavy-handed state support and direction focused on growth and top scores on economic indicators.

India and South Korea are both rumored to manipulate state currencies and have a heavy hand in industry; China is famous for it. Justin Yifu Lin, the former Chief Economist for the World Bank discusses the state's role in innovation and incubation:

> The state can also play a catalytic role in the development of new industries by incubation or attracting foreign direct investment, especially for entering industries where local firms have no past experience. The experience of successful Asian countries can be of relevance here. Because policymakers there understood that it would not be realistic or easy to enter a new industry about which their local firms had no historical knowledge, they used state institutions to encourage a gradual approach and promote joint-ventures: after the transition

to a market economy in the 1980s, China, for instance, initially set modest goals for its industrial development, and proactively invited direct investment from Hong Kong, Korea, Japan, and Taiwan. This promotion policy helped the local economy to get started in various industries. Bangladesh's vibrant garment industry also started with a Korean manufacturer's investment in Dhaka. After a few years, so much knowledge transfer had taken place that it became a sort of "incubation center". Not surprisingly, local garment plants mushroomed in Bangladesh, and almost each of them could be traced back to the Korean firm.[2]

There are many arguments for and against this form of state capitalism. Yasheng Huang has made brilliant points on China and state capitalism, all of which are valid when analyzing Chinese family offices and Chinese family office growth:

Advocates of state capitalism often cite China's high GDP growth as evidence of the efficacy of state capitalism. One problem with this view is that there has not been one growth model in China. There are at least two: one—prevailing in the 1980s and up to the mid-1990s—that is less statist in terms of the policy orientations and one since the mid-1990s that is increasingly rooted in state capitalism. GDP growth under both of these policy models has been robust. To say that state capitalism is responsible for China's fast GDP growth is to have committed an attribution error. The state never fully embraced privatization as a policy goal in and of itself. Privatization was intended as an instrument in the service of a larger goal. One way to characterize Chinese economy today is that it is an economic system rooted in "state capitalism." However, this characterization is not without controversy, both about whether the characterization is valid factually and/or whether the characterization entails prescriptive value for policy. Analysts who argue that China today is not state-capitalistic point to the private sector's large and growing shares of total output and employment. By the benchmark of commanding-heights economies, the size of the private sector in China is unremarkable.[3]

How remarkable is China's private-sector ownership? Studies and research have pegged the number all over the board, but it is safe to say that any Chinese company doing over $1 M in business in domestic China is taking on inexpensive state debt and most likely state ownership. There is a disagreement deep in the trenches and it is not surrounding defense or human rights but much more than that; it involves the ethos of the future which is being decided by multiple global powers. This is not Armageddon, but it is a

[2]New Structural Economics: A Framework for Rethinking Development. World Bank Group.

[3]Beloit College Upton Forum, The Annual Proceedings of The Wealth And Well-Being of Nations.

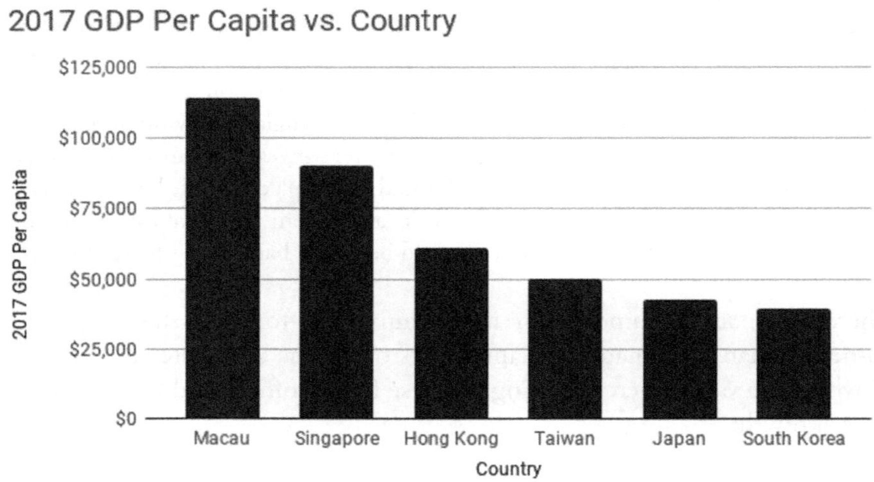

Fig. 5.1 Asia GDP per capita

reshaping of the world in multiple ways; from increased nationalism, anti-globalism, and policy and subsidy that supports domestic economics. One major point of contention is succession, as state intervention creates power vacuums with heirs and offsprings often not acting in lockstep with previous generations, therefore affecting mainland China-based business interests. As one can anticipate, the onslaught of Chinese family offices creating family office "funds" have banks in Asia intent on attracting mainland Chinese family office money for deployment offshore, meaning in nearby safer Asian markets (Fig. 5.1).

You cannot have a serious fortune in mainland China without being directly tied to the government. Mainland China has been making serious moves into the banking center. I first noticed this in the trading world when a friend's fund used CITIC as a prime broker in 2015. If you travel around Manhattan or London or San Francisco or Vancouver you will notice an increase in Asian banking branches:

> However, in the last few years, new banks from third countries have established their European hubs in Luxembourg, including the seven largest Chinese banks, including Bank of China, ICBC, the world's largest bank; Bank of Communications, Agricultural Bank of China, China Construction Bank, China Merchants Bank and China Everbright bank. In addition, many international banking groups are establishing competence centers in Luxembourg,

> either in private banking, fund administration, custodian services, in treasury management, or as booking centers for international loans.[4]

China is an exemplary example of interlocking industry within state and household. Ruled by the politburo—that is the officials of the Communist Party of China. The extent of China's control into private and public industry is unknown by the estimates but is far reaching. From analysis including Yasheng Huang's aforementioned paper, rough estimates peg 90% of all companies generating over 5 M yuan are state owned to some degree, whether this means something as simple as a low interest rate loan or complete state control we do not know. What is known is that China is very involved in the upper echelons of their economy and heads of industry are kept at an arm's length, if not in constant contact with government grandees. Additionally, it is very hard to find out what is what in China. Once you walk into medium- to large-sized businesses, you almost have to expect state debt or some state control, which delivers an extra conveyance of adherence.

The state has been expanding its banking practices in the mainland while simultaneously introducing new laws in Hong Kong.[5] Adopted on June 30, 2020, the new laws allow the extradition of Hongkongers to China and furthermore Article 38 of the law states that such law is applicable to every individual, including foreigners. Many have seen this as a deep subversion to the Sino-British Joint Declaration of 1984 and as result many financial businesses have downsized their firms' Hong Kong presence, established office in the mainland, or move regional capitals to places like Dubai or Singapore.

That aside Hong Kong can still remain an independent zone even if it is fully controlled by China. In the past few years Hong Kong's Securities and Futures Commission (SFC) organized new regulations for Open-Ended Fund Companies (OFC).

> The new OFC structure will allow investment funds to be set up in the form of a company, but with the flexibility for investors to trade the funds through the creation and cancellation of shares. This additional choice would help diversify Hong Kong's fund domiciliation platform and build up our fund manufacturing capabilities, which in turn would further develop Hong Kong's asset management industry. Under the OFC regime, the Securities and Futures Commission (SFC), being the principal regulator, is responsible for the registration and regulation of OFCs. The Registrar of Companies oversees the

[4]European Banking Federation 2019.

[5]Officially called: Law of the People's Republic of China on Safeguarding National Security in the Hong Kong Special Administrative Region.

incorporation and statutory corporate filings of OFCs and the Official Receiver the winding-up procedures.[6]

If we take the Open-Ended Fund Companies (OFC) model as an example perhaps a hybrid mix of Hong Kong-style Western market finance with heavy-handed mainland China regulation could synthesize the inland investor market and bring together the special administrative zones and offshoots like Taiwan with a centralized China–Hong Kong clearing system. If kept within Western financial parameters institutional investment could still be attracted to the east—if not grow more comfortable with the situation—a situation in which we could eventually expect to see all Chinese, Hong Kong, and Taiwanese companies listed in Western markets reorganizing and domiciling in China-controlled Hong Kong.

Hong Kong Exchanges and Clearing Limited, a global exchange and clearing concern, is the global market leader in many markets, especially Asia. HKEX operates four clearing houses in Hong Kong: Hong Kong Securities Clearing Company Limited (HKSCC), HKFE Clearing Corporation Limited (HKCC), the SEHK Options Clearing House Limited (SEOCH), and OTC Clearing Hong Kong Limited (OTC Clear) and owns the London Metal Exchange. In 2019 HKEX launched a failed bid for the London Stock Exchange, with the idea of creating the third largest exchange after NYSE and NASDAQ. Regardless, HKEX is now the world's largest exchange by way of listed company market capitalization of listed companies, with a total market cap of HK$47.52 trillion as of December 2020. [7]

Japan and South Korea

Japan, South Korea, Mainland China, and Hong Kong have similar elements of ruling families controlling important elements of industry. In Japan, before the wars, a form of management and ownership called a Zaibatsu uniformly controlled economic activities and trading. Always family-owned and controlled, the Zaibatsu were interlocking and led to cartel domination. The groups lent to each other, opened new business on behalf of each other, and coexisted as a family-dominated industrial complex. As the Zaibatsu were dismantled after the war, they partially dissolved and partially formed into a modern example called *the keiretsu*. It is through the Keiretsu the history

[6]Companies House, Hong Kong Special Administrative Region.

[7]"HKEX soars to become world's largest exchange operator by market cap". *South China Morning Post*. 21 July 2020.

of the vertically integrated Zaibatsu lives on. Additionally, Japan has a type of company—sogo shosha—which emerged after the temporary shutdown and partial structure of Japan's economy after World War II. These sogo shosha companies (which mean a general trading company) emerged from the ashes of the larger Zaibatsu, into vertical or horizontal Keiretsu members. Mitsubishi, Mitsui & Co., Itochu, Sojitz, and Toyota Tsusho are but a few.

The modern Keiretsu is either horizontal or vertical in integration, let's look at Mitsubishi for clarity. The Mitsubishi Group is made up of about 40 individual companies without a controlling parent company. Each of the Mitsubishi companies owns substantial (but usually not controlling) portions of the shares of the others.

Korea's similar system is a chaebol. The system is very powerful and controls almost all the businesses and enterprises in South Korea from LCD televisions to iron and steel making for ocean liners to entertainment. Earlier in the decade South Korea fined LCD TV makers for price fixing, and a number of former state presidents and families have been imprisoned for corruption and bribery in the past years. South Korea and North Korea have an improving relationship, and North Korea has yet again been brought to the national stage.

The Indian Subcontinent

In India, socialism emerged after the Russian Revolution and took route when Nehru took over as prime minister. Today a modern mixed economy persists, with elements of state capitalism and traditional capitalism. A long history of trade and merchant activity, India since the 1950s has been in a socialist reform with devastating effects. Capitalist and merchant behavior derived great wealth over an expansive continent post-British rule. It also led to a bit of a land grab and opportunity grab with fierce competition and a system of corruption prevalent in many ways. On another note fortunes from India are often multigenerational and take some time to build, and the new ones are learning from their older and wiser counterparts.

The modern Indian economy first opened up in 1991. Since independence from Britain, India is blighted by corruptions and false starts. Right-wing nationalism from groups and movements such as Hindutva—a Hindu call to arms and nationalism—to the opposite side is taking shape. However there is no shortage of affluent citizens. The country is massive and each region has specialization and relationships with other parts of the world; Chennai is home to many firms, as historically it housed part of the East India Company, and Bengaluru, in the Karnataka region is home to notable global firms like Reuters (reporting often comes from the Bangalore bureau). However this specialization differs from Delhi, Hyderabad, Mumbai, and Gujarat, the latter bordering Pakistan with a substantial merchant trade.

Nehru wanted a planned economy which created enormous red tape often called the License Raj, and over time that inefficiency led to a deeply mixed economy, with state control, state monopolies, plutocrats, and staggering inequality. On the latter, inequality has only become more of a problem with the share of income going to the 1% and the 0.1% having doubled since 1991.[8] There is no doubt in mind that India will become a major world player in the next few decades, including a booming middle class which should have profound effects on India and the region as a whole. Whatever growing pains India is fumbling with, eventually those growing pains will mature. India was one of the first rural economies to develop a robust mobile network, and their state technical school is often chosen by students over American ivy league universities. I have been curious about the Indian middle class for some time now. Abhijit Roy, a Professor of Marketing at the Kania School of Management, University of Scranton summarizes the forecast of India's middle class for the Association of Asian Studies below:

> India's population continues to grow rapidly—by 2022, it is expected to surpass China's, according to a United Nations report. The middle-class population in the country is expected to grow rapidly in the next decade, and by 2027, the size of this group is expected to be larger than that of China, the United States, and Europe. According to current projections, India's share of world GDP will increase substantially from 7.6 percent in 2017 to 8.5 percent of the world share in 2020, and to further accelerate to 475 million by 2030, hence having more middle-class consumers than China by that time. The global middle class is expected to grow significantly until 2030, with a significant number of people from India moving into this group. The expansion of the middle class in India will not only enhance domestic consumption but also continue to grow the country's outbound tourism. By 2020, this sector is expected to exceed US $40 billion and be close to $45 billion in 2022.[9]

While the concept of family offices may be new on the Indian continent there are plenty of Indian billionaires and millionaires scattered throughout the world. As one can only imagine, a fair amount of Indian fortunes have found their way into London. Many have branch offices in the United States as well, however with the travel distance between India and the Unites States,

[8]India Economics, Figures from Zermatt Credit Research / HCG Companies.

[9]The Middle Class in India, Abbit Roy. Association for Asian Studies. 2018.

families that opt to put their family office in London or continental Europe are able to stay connected to the mainland much easier due to the semi-shared cultural aspects and ease of travel.

There is a set of economists who believe India to be a plutocracy. I do not foresee global family office investing in Mumba's Stock Exchange anytime soon, but I do foresee a continuation of establishing family offices and family investments in India, throughout the continent. The government in India is concerned about money leaking into the offshore. India uses Seychelles and Mauritius as a tax haven almost exclusively due to the proximity.

India has a massive population and the majority of its inhabitants speak Hindu. However, in India you also have over twenty major languages, thirteen alphabets, and a reported five hundred regional dialects. Roughly one-third to half the population speaks Hindi, but consolidating the others has never been done and likely will never be done. In each of the regions they have unique caste systems and they are often engrained in the psyche of citizens.

Thailand is one of the next booming markets and the family dynamics are culturally unique. You have the Crown Property Bureau (CPB). Established in the 1937, the CPB was initially under the Bureau of the Royal Household, the Bureau of the Royal household is similar to the British royal family's household office and continental ducal European offices. Recently, King Maha Vajiralongkorn has taken ownership of the assets—now the King will be taxed on the billions in assets. The CPB is a worthwhile institution to study because it encompasses vast planning in a part of the world as well as encompassing elements of the Sufficiency Economy (SE) which is mentioned in later chapters.

Australia has an interesting economy and a long history of family businesses and family ownership within large industrial assets, however many of the current family offices in Australia are in their first generation of formation. The country is also very adept at trade; and they have a sophisticated capital market ecosystem to further support their economies. Australia's booming FOs population is widely centered on the wealthier areas of the island continent, which is heavily centered in Melbourne and Sydney. Apart from the very famous Aussie fortunes like the Packer and Murdoch family, Australia has a robust economy and Australia has substantial trade relations with most of the globe, let alone the nearby region. New Zealand is much the same. Both countries rank high on global wealth lists and both countries rank especially high in the breakdown of wealth per adult. Both are adept at trade and have liberal common sense economies.

The recent IMDB scandal which embroiled the 6th Prime Minister of Malaysia (2009–2018) has been a stain on the industry and the region. Police seized 1400 necklaces, 567 handbags, 423 watches, 2200 rings, 1600 brooches, and 14 tiaras worth $273 million. This was the material wealth they found, not the bank accounts and financial instruments and private investments. I am unaware if this includes bank accounts and holdings in Malaysia's associated offshore zone, Labuan. Indonesia and Malaysia are predominately Muslim countries with Islamic statutes in the constitution but both countries have a long history of toleration. Malaysia has a separate Sharia Court (for Muslims only) and Article 160 of the Constitution of Malaysia applies a certain definition of what it is to be a Malay person, under Article 160 a Malay must be Islamic, in addition to other observed customs. A non-Muslim who wishes to marry a Muslim in Malaysia must convert to Islam. It is important to note that both Indonesia and Malaysia have substantial non-Muslim populations, with the eastern region of Indonesia, Papua being predominately of the Protestant religion. Indonesia has the largest Muslim population in the world with over 200 M of the population being Muslim, compromising more than 80% of the country.[10]

Singapore separated from Malaysia in the 1960s and has since followed its own path of development. Singapore, the undeniable leader in Asia Pacific finance is equally poised to be the family office capital. If an Asian family has a family office, and if that FO is to have a branch office, it is more than often in Singapore. As mentioned Singapore is the de facto hub for many Asian family offices. Before the FOs practice exploded in popularity Hong Kong and Asia's other regionalized metropolis were standard, but the high concentration of top shelf services and strong local law have driven Singapore to the top. In Asia the location of your family office is also vital. Singapore has become a popular choice, as it is a well-regulated international financial center and wealth management hub located in the heart of Asia. Furthermore, offshore income is, by and large, not taxed and onshore income is often lowly taxed due to Singapore's territorial tax system. There is also no capital gains tax nor inheritance tax.

Singapore is poised to become the Asian hub for SFOs and MFOs, as I have discussed earlier. Hong Kong still has a great foothold, as does Taipei, but Singapore is growing substantially, especially in the world of fund management and family offices where Singapore is attracting attention from regional powerhouses like Australia, and with the very wealthy families through the whole of Asia Pacific.

[10] Figures from Zermatt Credit Research / HCG Companies.

Recently, the Monetary Authority of Singapore (MAS) has established a new framework for funds that fall into the category of: Variable Capital Company (VCC). I have included a brief explanation of the VCC scheme from the MAS.

> Variable Capital Company framework from the Monetary Authority of Singapore (MAS):
>
> Provide greater flexibility. A VCC can be used by both open-ended and closed-end investment funds, and for both traditional and alternative strategies. It can also pay dividends using its capital.
>
> Achieve cost efficiencies. The umbrella structure creates economies of scale as sub-funds can share the same board of directors and common service providers and consolidate some administrative functions.
>
> Cater to the needs of global investment funds. A VCC will be permitted to use Singapore and international accounting standards (such as the International Financial Reporting Standards and US Generally Accepted Accounting Principles) in preparing financial statements so that it can serve the needs of global investors.
>
> Enhance safeguards. The VCC framework provides safeguards against the commingling of assets and liabilities between sub-funds, by requiring assets and liabilities of each sub-fund to be segregated. As such, the assets of one sub-fund may not be used to discharge the liabilities of another sub-fund, or of the umbrella fund, including in the event of insolvency.[11]

There is a boom in families setting up family office funds in Singapore, as well as establishing funds which are really funds owned and managed by family offices. This is important to note as Asia is very active in the trading world—from new issues to robust futures contracts in multiple markets—and Singapore is no exception. Indonesia on the other hand is closely related to Singapore and also in deep development mode. The government has long been in talks to transfer their capital from Jakarta to another part of the country, possibly the eastern provinces. One reason could be staggering growth. Jakarta, Bangkok, and Manilla have been enjoying year-over-year growth, and creating new wealth, from a richer agricultural class and middle class to the newly minted rich. Outside of China this is where the growing super rich may be found next, and with that you have the next wave of family offices. Indonesia is a diverse country with a rich history with a multitude of nationalities. I foresee the wealth being created staying in Indonesia and

[11]MAS introduces new corporate structure to enhance fund ecosystem in Singapore, Monetary Authority of Singapore, 10 September 2018.

overtime creating a well-developed nation that mirrors Singapore but also operating as one of many Islamic finance hubs.

The Business of Inheritance

Inherences in Asia greatly differ with region and territory. As discussed earlier Japan and Korea hold a dizzying amount of interlaced corporate structures. This is no different in family offices and family businesses. In Japan and Korea commerce, historically, has been under control by powerful families with interlocking ownership. While this has morphed into new practices since the 1950s, it has been slow to overhaul. Family offices exist but families are so accustomed to being major shareholders of medium to large corporates—directly—that many of these companies have only now begun to ratify their conflicts of interest within the ownership suite.

The Chearavanont family is a family of Bangkok billionaires. Dhanin Chearavanont (also known as Chia Kok Min) and his brothers own the Charoen Pokphand Group, a massive international conglomerate. They are the sons of Chia Ek Chor, who founded CP in 1921 in Bangkok. CP Group partnered with the Continental Grain in 1981 to enter the Chinese market, which marked the opening of the first foreign-owned feed mill in China. CP Group is private but owns a vast array of companies, some private and some public on numerous stock exchanges. The family owns the license for 7-Eleven and KFC in Thailand. They also own Ping Ang, which is the largest insurance company in the world by market cap. Companies they own are in multiple countries and listed in multiple currencies. They are by their very nature a family of international billionaires, like it or not. Reclusive by native, Dhanin has been the most senior to be active.

The family is portrayed as independent from the company operations for the most part, a company that employs hundreds of thousands of employees. Dhanin and his siblings Jaran Chiaravanont, Montri Jiaravanont and Sumet Jiaravanon, all spell their names differently. Danin and his brothers also decided the succession dynamics in CP group; keeping the children out of controlling the agriculture aspects but controlling other assets like hypermarkets (7-Eleven) and communications and depending on the setup of a family office to provide for the other generations.

The upcoming generations, like many others in similar situations, have other business interests and the vision of the leaders was to create further separation from ownership and management; the vehicle of a family office was perfect to oversee such issues.

Family offices have been slow to take in Asia pacific, but a recent development has been the creation of family-owned investment funds. A look at Hong Kong's IPO markets and the offshore worlds closely reveal a massive amount of money flow and investment. Research shows that family-held businesses in Asia lose significant value when transitioning to the next generation. Some find it easier—and more profitable—to sell. That could explain the influx of cash into Honk Kong and Singapore family groups. There is a lot more trading going on in Asia Pacific and the trend is moving east. Families also may gather large positions by owning equity in the listed companies they in fact list, thereby running internal hedge strategies and fund behavior.

What Asia lacks in the FOs' sector it makes up for as a whole with planning and forward thinking. Asia has a history of succession, and previous practices of succession are worth researching for worthwhile applications. The Asian plan well—generally. If they need to go offshore Japan has the Cook Islands and Labuan, Malaysian. The Labuan offshore financial services authority (The first step in formulating a legitimate financial services industry in an offshore center is to establish a monetary authority). Regardless, in 1997, the prime minister of Malaysia stated by 2020 the area would be industrialized and modern. It still has quite a way to go but this shows some development in a largely Islamic rule country. In Asia it is not uncommon for a son-in-law to take over the in-laws company and be legally adopted, and change what is referred to as a surname. That happened countless times in Europe and the United States, and it would still happen if inheritance laws and social customs called for it.

Case Study: The Ambani Family

One of the more famous inheritance battles of modern India was between the Ambani family. Tycoon Dhirubhai Ambani, having suffered a series of health setbacks, has been relinquishing control of Reliance Industries to his sons, Anil and Mukesh. In 2002 Dhirubhani died without a will, and things took a turn for the worse.

The brothers had many disagreements and separated the companies in 2005, one for Mukesh and one for Anil. Mukesh took control of Reliance Industries Limited (petroleum, chemicals, entertainment) and Anil took control of Reliance Anil Dhirubhai Ambani Group, commonly known as Reliance Group (telecom and electrical power). As of June 2020 Anil is worth roughly \$9B, Mukesh over \$44B. Both groups have grown and collected accolades, but Mukesh has become the richest man in all of Asia, even surpassing Jack Ma.

Mukesh's standout performance was initially led by his commodities business and then a telecom concern, Reliance Jio Infocomm Limited (Jio), which he debuted in 2007. Jio soon swept up all the competition, including his own brother Anil. As Anil suffered business setbacks his brother eventually came to the rescue, seemingly healing the family rift. Regardless, the families command of economics and business acumen is best in class.

Bibliography

"The Four Little Dragons", Ezra F. Vogel. 1991. Details in works cited.

See New Structural Economics: A Framework for Rethinking Development. World Bank Group.

Beloit College Upton Forum, The Annual Proceedings of The Wealth And Well-Being of Nations.

European Banking Federation 2019.

Officially called: Law of the People's Republic of China on Safeguarding National Security in the Hong Kong Special Administrative Region.

Companies House, Hong Kong Special Administrative Region.

Figures from Zermatt Credit Research / HCG Companies internal geographic reports.

MAS introduces new corporate structure to enhance fund ecosystem in Singapore, Monetary Authority of Singapore, 10 September 2018.

6

Family Office Investing

In this chapter I am going to discuss a few large family offices that have controlled important market segments in their respective businesses through multigenerational ownership and strategic investing. I will also discuss direct investing in family offices and common themes surrounding family office investing.

Family Commodities: Cargill, Continental Grain Company & Seaboard

A tremendous modern example of families in action can be directed to Continental Grain Co., known as CGC or ContiGrain. Continental Grain Company was founded in 1813 in Arlon, Belgium. Conti's history is filled with landmarks complete from the first firm to trade with the Soviets and also with China; opening the first foreign-owned operations with Charoen Pokphand (Thailand) and holding—quite possibly—the first business license granted by China when China first allowed foreign corporates to invest. They have also stayed at the forefront, divesting and reorganizing and returning to the fold, albeit a new fold, by recently investing in "sustainable food technology including Impossible Foods, the plant-based burger company, and Modern Meadow, which grows cell-based leather."[1] While Conti formerly

[1] Continental Grain (CGC) www.continentalgrain.com/culture/heritage/.

C. Hagan, *Global Family Office Investing*,
https://doi.org/10.1007/978-3-030-18224-3_6

had expansive industrial assets for grain trading, over time they sold the grain elevators to Cargill and shuffled the operation around. In due time Conti pivoted back into foods, but this time as an investor, investing with 3G Capital and other strategic which led to their subsequent participation in some of the larger deals of the past decade including Burger King (2010), H.J. Heinz Company (2013); the roll up of Tim Hortons and Burger King to Restaurants Brands International (2014), and the merger of H.J. Heinz Company and Kraft Foods Group forming the Kraft Heinz Company (2015). In October of 2018 Bunge Limited added Paul J. Fribough—Chairman and CEO of CGC—to the board of directors of the multifamily-owned international grain trading house Bunge Limited. This was brought on by CGC's campaign with other prominent hedge funds to force change at Bunge. CGC also invested into Castleton, a former energy division of another storied agriculture trading company owned by the Louis-Dreyfus family.

CGC, Cargill, and Seaboard

Arlon, which is CGC's private equity unit and also the name of the families' European town they originated from, has $1.5B under assets. One of the reasons I am centering on CGC is from their reinvention. CGC has investments and partnerships with Seaboard. Seaboard was founded nearly 100 years ago by Otto Bresky and by nature of their influence in the ag and commodity space they have been rubbing shoulders with giants for some time—they are not bona fide giants themselves. The fortunes of Seaboard are nailed to the whims of commodity prices but hedging and information on their side, when the times are good they are abnormally profitable. The Seaboard portfolio is robust with 2015 net sales clocking in at over $6B. It includes a massive array of companies with which it has tremendous operations in pork, shrimp, and salmon (through aquaculture) and commodity trading and processing. They have companies all over the world in the broadest sense of the word. The family-led firm is now led by heir Steven Bresky, who like the other family members prefers to stay out of the press.

Seaboard sold its milling operations to Cargill in the 1980s. It is worthwhile to note the antitrust analysis that went into Conti's divestment of assets to Cargill. Continental unloaded a substantial amount of assets and client accounts, the transaction included grain logistics and trading infrastructures in 30 countries and a large customer base. Many of these locations controlled substantial market share in the local grain and oilseed markets.

I have included a scholarly discourse on the sale of a Conti unit to Cargill International in 1999. The transaction hit the radar of the Department of Justice and triggered many complaints. The breadth of industry coverage is staggering to comprehend as it touched logistics, pricing, and perhaps other security.

> If approved by the DOJ, the assets and selected employees will be transferred in the first quarter, 1999. In the U.S., Cargill indicates that these assets include 83 grain handling facilities, which will add 73 new locations to their current 243, and 10 facilities where Continental and Cargill elevators currently coexist close to each other. Cargill and Continental are important in other parts of the world grain economy as well. For example, a Cargill Argentina press release indicates the combined operations would account for about 25 percent of Argentine com wheat and soybean exports. They are significant competitors in most areas of grain production, along with such trading companies and merchandisers such as Peavey, ADM, Bunge, Zen Noh, Cenex Harvest States, Tradigrain, Farmland, AGP, Nidera, Mitsui, Marubeni, Mitsubishi, Kanematsu, Glencore, Oriac, Itochu, CAM, A.C. Toepfer, and Seaboard.

As one can only imagine for the families to create such an elaborate and important commodity system it took generations and generations of hard work and educated investments. Needless to say, this was more than any business school case study could ever hope for, this was powerful market influence that had the ability to affect every person in the globe, without exaggerating much. This behemoth was merely Conti's grain merchandising portfolio, and Conti was one of the largest exporters and traders of grain in the world. They had centuries of success in grain trading under wraps and managed to leave the business right before market data and grain pricing would disseminate to retail investors and local farmers, threatening their lucrative margins. The fortitudes of all the generations are highly admirable. Cargill on the other hand is another study for another book, but I will briefly detail the Cargill clan.

Apart from Cargill buying Conti's grain unit and also being a private concern like Conti, the family shareholders of the extended family compile some of the wealthiest families in the world. For years and years the upper leadership of Cargill Inc. was based on Lake Minnetonka in a stately mansion that had been converted into executive offices. Over the past few years the executives have departed, moving to the main company headquarters in Minnetonka. One of the reasons for the departure was the fact that it was too secretive, adding tenfold to the mystique in the fireplace-laden chateau. Founded by William Wallace Cargill in 1865, William was soon joined by his brothers, and in time in-laws and extended family. Cargill was originally formed in Conover, Iowa when William bought a flat house for grain. Conover is now a ghost town, but it was close to the family home in Janesville, Wisconsin. Modern Janesville includes a great deal of Cargill namesake from a church to a day care but the company has long since departed and grown into a super power. The headquarters was placed in La Crosse, Wisconsin, because it was a railroad meeting point (Milwaukee connected to Southern Minnesota Railroad). In 1895 John H. McMillian married Edna Clara Cargill and the two families were joined together formally—there were neighbors in La Crosse. Eventually the Macmillan descendants would reach equal prominence in the enterprise from merits and inheritance. The fate of Cargill followed the railroad in the early days, and by 1942 they were making steel-hulled ocean vessels at "Port Cargill" the south of Minneapolis on the riverways. The company continued to make barges for river transporting of grain and eventually received an award for service from the Armed Forces. The case: Bunge Corporation v Tradex Export SA (1981)[2] is a well-read case law in England on contractual obligations. Tradex was established by Cargill to handle their international interests and Bunge, as mentioned, is an international agricultural dynasty that is now publicly traded with Paul Fribourg of Continental Grain as an activist investor and board member.

Cargill has since diversified into salt, protein, and fertilizer, to name a few. They had a hedge fund unit which was phased out, Black River Asset Management, but that was rumored to have been influential and created a positive ripple effect on the local asset management and capital markets business in Minneapolis. Cargill now allocates, and has a shareholder family office, in addition to other decentralized family offices as one would expect from a $36B shared fortune.

JAB Holding Company

Perhaps one of the largest private companies you have never heard of, JAB, is a food brand and commodity giant. Conti CGC also teamed up with JAB as JAB pivoted to center on coffee and food, away from luxury products. CGC has been a partner with JAB since 2014, joining as an investor right around the time JAB funds purchased and rolled up numerous companies—their portfolio includes household names in the food and coffee sector including,

[2]Bunge Corporation (New York) v Tradax Export SA (Panama) [1981] UKHL 11 (25 February 1981).

but not limited to: Douwe Egberts, Gevalia, Stumptown Coffee Roaster, Peet's Coffee & Tea, Keurig Green Mountain, Krispy Kreme Doughnuts, Einstein Bros. Bagels, and Panera Bread, Caribou, and Dr. Pepper—Snapple (a unit of Keurig). JAB has been on a buying spree—even buying the British sandwich and coffee shop Pre A Manger for $2B in May of 2018. JAB owns a 37% stakes in Coty, a brand conglomerate owning over a tremendous amount of famous names fragrance and cosmetic brands (Adidas, Lacoste, Calvin Klein) notably larger now since P&G sold off 43 brands to Coty in 2015 for some $12B. It should be noted that over the past five years JAB has been increasing their investment in Coty.

JAB operates in a different manner and has floated bonds in Luxembourg through JAB Holdings B.V on the Luxembourg Stock Exchange. They also at times require special terms of trade. JAB is overseen by a small group of partners who sit on associated company boards or lead the investments directly in an interlocking system (to a degree). They are active managers and majority investors. JAB also has a very large footprint with offices on three continents (the United States, South America, and Europe) and it seems few family members, if any are involved in the day-to-day management of the enterprise.

Johann A. Benckiser GmbH, the investment vehicle of the Reimann family which is now called JAB Holding Company is aggressively targeting coffee and food companies. In the past few years, JAB has purchased Panera, the Panera rival Au Bon Pain (and their centralized baking operations) and Pret A Manger. The pivot from luxury to commodity food brands has been successful, and with the perceived method of vertical integration and multiple large-scale production points there is a chance JAB will become more profitable than ever before.

In February of this year, it was announced that JAB may take their coffee division public. The coffee portfolio is sectioned into a group known as Acorn, which also holds three groups and their respected brands. I have attempted to list the components of each group below:

Keurig Dr Pepper

- Tully's Coffee
- Van Houtte
- Green Mountain
- Keurig
- The original Donut Shop Coffee
- Dr Pepper
- Snapple
- Cananda Dry

- Schweppes
- 7Up

JDE (Jacobs Douwe Egberts)

- Jacobs
- Gevalia
- Pilao
- Kenco
- Moccona
- Douwe Egberts

Peet's Coffee

- Stumptown
- Intelligentsia
- Mighty Leaf
- Peet's Coffee & Tea

Bear in mind that this list leaves out other holdings and just represents the collected brands in "Acord Holdings," which is a portfolio inside JAB. The other holdings of JAB are Panera Holding, Krispy Kreme, Coty, Reckitt Benckiser, and JAB Luxury.

Reckitt Benckiser is the behemoth with over 35,000 employees and $14B in sales.

Today Reckitt Benckiser Group Plc manufactures household, health, and personal care products. Geographically segmented into regions which cover the globe including: Europe and North America (ENA); Latin America, North Asia, South East Asia and Australia and New Zealand (LAPAC); and Russia and CIS, Middle East, North Africa, Turkey, and Sub-Saharan Africa (RUMEA). Reckitt Benckiser owns such well known brands as include Airborne, MegaRed, Clearasil, Woolite, and Varnish. This is the core of the Reimann family fortune, a fortune that began in 1823 when Johann A Benckiser created Benckiser, which would go on to become Reckitt Benckiser. The modern-day Reimann family was in the formation of Reckitt Benckiser early history; in 1928, five years after Johann founded Benckiser, Ludwig Reimann joined the firm and married into the family. Today it is the children, grandchildren and great-grandchildren of Ludwig Reimann's great-grandson, Albert Reimann, Jr. who own about 90% of JAB Holdings, along with Agnaten SE a principle holding company domiciled in Austria. Of course, these could change at any moment, and are pursuant to JAB's management but I imagine due to the every developing public–private ownership system JAB is venturing into, one can assume this will largely stay the same. I am unaware of the Reimann family SFO structures, as it is my experience that families as tremendously wealthy as the Reimann's utilize many single family offices, foundations, trusts and family owned trust companies or banks.

American Apparel (in Bankruptcy)

I was involved directly in the American Apparel takeover attempts of 2015 and 2016. I had seized an opportunity to directly invest in the takeover in early December 2015.

Bottom line is: I worked directly with Dov Charney and the financier David Felman in Los Angeles to take over American Apparel between December 2015 and February 2016. The saga had been playing out for some time in the headlines for a variety of reasons. Needless to say, we were not expecting such an array of the press; we were merely trophy hunting—going after large deals using leveraged finance.

I had become familiar with American Apparel in college from their advertisements in Harvard Square so I was aware of the brand as it matured, and ultimately followed their developments as a professional investor. By the time we connected Dov had become a cultural icon in many ways, so I knew that the company had the ability to ebb and flow, due to the entrepreneur industrialist at the helm. Additionally, I noticed early on that Mr. Charney had a genius-like command of the world of advertising, massmedia, and public relations. At the time he had the ability to communicate through countless mediums in a way that seem absolutely effortless but yet remained incredibly effective.

The first time I began tracking American Apparel from a professional analysis point of view was in 2009 when Lion Capital invested. I tracked American Apparel for over five years. One morning in November or December of 2015 I was up early on a weekend, preparing research for the holiday months. My wife and I had been in our new house for about six months and I was still setting up my home office. I had my news terminal running and a headline about American Apparel popped up on the screen. It was about 8 am EST. I emailed the contacts listed in the press release and later that day I was put in immediate touch with Dov. Soon we were on Facetime and within the same day we were formulating a term sheet.

Within a few weeks Martin Bienenstock of Proskauer had agreed to represent our family office on the deal, and the press began to heat up. Bienenstock came highly recommended and has in the past represented the W. R. Grace ad hoc shareholders' committee; General Motors in Chapter 11 case; Enron Corporation in Chapter 11; Caesars Entertainment (unsecured claimholders' committee); Westinghouse (statutory creditors' committee) as well as serving on the Financial Oversight and Management Board for Puerto Rico.

My father, Bob Hagan, largely stayed out of the mechanics but expected updates and warned about accruing egregious legal fees, and our in-house counsel (Richard Feldman) basically did the same. Legal estimates for fighting this out in Delaware bankruptcy court for Hagan Capital was north of $4M, with $2M in escrow immediately if we chose to pursue a fight. Egregious legal fees aside we were equalled as surprised at how much press was flying around. I had to keep my mobile phone on silent for fear of accidentally picking up the phone and having a fashion blogger on the other end firing off questions.

On the deal, Jim Eppelin and I handled the bulk of work, with a few analysts and partners, which included two additional SFOs and an external CPA, Tracy D. Barrett. From the start of the analysis we were very focused on supply chains and the steps it took to bring textiles to market; from cotton to weaving and dying and cutting. David Felman, Dov's investment banker, organized a set of terms and a substantial plan to recap the group. Over the next few weeks the original investment plans would triple in size.

The family business and ultimately family office world in which I came from called for out-of-the-box thinking. I did not find Dov unusual or threatening. Dov had a hard-driving entrepreneurial attitude, and we were completely focused on taking back an empire he had created, so hearing the inside knowledge from him was as befuddling to me to hear as it was for him to be fighting for his enterprise. There was a serious corporate history here and by that I mean economic history. At this time the company was still headquartered in its famous downtown LA factory, with a vertically integrated model.

Here is the second bid term sheet, edited and condensed:

January 7, 2016

Letter Sent To Creditors By Hagan Capital Group and Cardinal Advisors:

Ladies and Gentlemen:

We are pleased to submit this follow-up third non-binding proposal for American Apparel, Inc. (the "Proposal") following our letters dated December 7, 2015 and December 29, 2015 and pursuant to the letter from Moelis & Company dated December 13, 2015. This Proposal summarizes the principal terms of a proposed acquisition (the "Transaction") of American Apparel, Inc., a Delaware Corporation, and all of its subsidiaries and related U.S. and non-U.S. companies including but not limited to the following entities that filed voluntary Chapter 11 petitions on October 5, 2015: American Apparel

(USA), LLC, American Apparel Retail, Inc., American Apparel Dyeing & Finishing, Inc., KCL Knitting, LLC and Fresh Air Freight, Inc. (collectively, "American Apparel", the "Company" or the "Debtor"), pursuant to which the entity signing below, or another entity to be formed for the purpose of this Transaction (collectively, the "Buyer" or "we"), will acquire the Company. This Indication is not binding and is conditioned on the completion of definitive documentation satisfactory to all parties. We are submitting this Proposal to you; its existence and terms are strictly confidential and shall be treated as such and shall not be disclosed or discussed by you with any other party, except with the Company, the Senior Lenders (as defined below), and the Unsecured Creditors Committee, and their respective legal and financial advisors who need to know the contents hereof in connection with our discussions concerning the proposed Transaction and who agree, or who are otherwise legally required, to keep such contents confidential. The specific terms of our Proposal are as follows:

We are submitting this Proposal to you; its existence and terms are strictly confidential and shall be treated as such and shall not be disclosed or discussed by you with any other party, except with the Company, the Senior Lenders (as defined below), and the Unsecured Creditors Committee, and their respective legal and financial advisors who need to know the contents hereof in connection with our discussions concerning the proposed Transaction and who agree, or who are otherwise legally required, to keep such contents confidential.

We believe our Proposal should be highly compelling to the Company and the Senior Lenders, providing the following benefits to the Company and its stakeholders as compared to the current Debtor plan:

a. Maximum long-term viability of the Company and value to its stakeholders including its over 8,500 employees with (i) seasoned industry and company veterans identified to quickly turnaround the Company, and (ii) the cooperation of and no ongoing open business competition from Mr. Dov Charney.
b. Improved recovery to the Senior Lenders vs. the Debtor plan. Assuming a $225 million total enterprise value (the midpoint of the Debtor's valuation range), the Senior Lenders would have an estimated recovery of 58% under their proposed plan through their equity conversion. The Senior Lenders will have a higher estimated recovery of 154% under our Proposal, and through a more senior security interest.
c. Improved liquidity and capitalization of the reorganized Company including $90 million of equity cushion and an expected $50 million ABL facility (undrawn at close). Total liquidity including cash, revolver availability and equity cushion is estimated to be $160 million at exit under our Proposal, which compares to $80 million under the Debtor plan.
d. An attractive valuation to the Debtor, significantly above the high end of the Debtor's stated valuation range of $180 to $270 million as provided in the

Debtor's Disclosure Statement. e. No ongoing requirements for the Senior Lenders to invest further capital into the Company, which their Plan shows as approximately $130 million of capital. Our Proposal also fully cashes out the existing DIP Facility.

e. Improved recovery to the unsecured creditors of approximately 20% of their aggregate claims, as compared to approximately 2% under the Debtor plan.

We well understand the inner workings of the recent declines of the Company and we are convinced that we are best equipped to return the Company to the growth trajectory it was on prior to the founder's departure. Despite the 2015 year to date (through September 30th) declines in net sales and gross profit of 15.5% and 29.2%, respectively, our team is energized about the long-term strategic opportunities of American Apparel, and we believe we are well positioned to turn around the Company. We fully believe that this Proposal is the best solution and a win-win for all parties involved – providing improved recoveries to the Senior Lenders while, with our exit capital structure, team, and vision, maximizing the long-term viability of the Company and the long-run value to its stakeholders.

The Turn Around Plan

A series of conference calls with the current management team—some pleasant, some horrific—were held with all the teams involved. What resulted was a long back and forth and then a complete freeze out due to our involvement with Dov. I think we fired off three term sheets in total. The controlling interests would not have anything to do with Dov Charney and they relayed that message many times.

From a long-term perspective, the bid for American Apparel made a lot of sense. We had Dov and he had the inside knowledge. This was a huge value add and it is not unusual—from a turnaround perspective—to reinstall a founder in a failing company. It has been known to work. Despite the issues management had before, we felt Dov had the energy and vision to get American Apparel back on track.

From our perspective Dov was going to be installed as a Co-CEO, with another industry leader. Due to the controversy, additional arrangements would have to be made and limitations would be put in place. CEOs can often get away with erratic and irrational behavior when the company is making money, but as soon as revenue falters the scrutiny begins. We had prepared a shortlist of potential executives, including reinstating many of the former executives and managers who had departed or were wrongfully terminated.

Almost all of the risk was headline risk and by that I mean a risk of the press turning against us or the deal going south with us handcuffed to a sinking ship. We maybe had a few millions in fees if we could penetrate the veil and get a hold of the enterprise, but the reality of this came and went rather quickly.

I have long followed Gerald M. Loeb's quote: Listen to everyone, follow no one. Loeb was a financier who pioneered financial journalism. He was an ardent analyst, and instilled a style of travel and living as an investor: analysis in everyday life and actions. We were going after the basics. American Apparel was just that—to consumers it was deeply connected from the advertisements—but really just a vertically integrated basics company. There was importing, weaving, and dying involved. Both sides—Hagan Capital and Dov's team—had intense plans. The stores in South Korea and the United Kingdom were profitable. I think Germany was profitable too. One of the backup plans we had was to close the underperforming US stores and reposition them into a new model. At the time Uniqlo had a flagship store in Manhattan with a very meaningful communication system which did a very good job nagging the consumer and educating the consumer on the virtues of their company. American Apparel had high marks within ESG principles and global awareness. As discussed in this book, ESG is a popular qualifier in capital markets. We were very hopeful on the turnaround assuming we could secure ownership of the company with a manageable debt burden.

The short-term opportunity was at least \$700M in revenue and EBITA of \$65M with projections of revenue over \$1B and EBITA north of \$100M. We could foreseeably hit the \$1B mark if we slimmed down the large real estate footprint to a flagship NYC store, a few LA stores, and keeping the ones in South Korea, Germany, and the United Kingdom. It was clear we could cut the abundance of payroll, inventory, and therefore production, and realize immediate savings. SKU's and inventory were set to be reduced by 30%. If we scaled up wholesale (which accounted for almost half the revenue); if we limited expenses and cleaned up supply chain, with American Apparel's massive content collection, we would have a brand with a legacy that we could into \$1B territory within five years. In 2014 numbers, represented in the American Apparel, Inc. FORM 8-B filed June 08, 2015 for the period ending June 08, 2015 American Apparel had 242 stores, \$609M net sales, and 10,000 employees. It was the largest vertical integrated manufacturer in America.

I was called as a witness in the bankruptcy case. It was quite an experience as the case was heavily followed. The premise of the case was the opinion from our side that Moelis & Co. has not been fair and transparent with the transaction. We were frozen out of the deal. I can attest to that—information was partially made available, and then made available, etc. There was a lot of tension between the American Apparel management team and Dov and that led to a lot of obstacles, as one could expect.

While I cannot claim responsivity for the idea of a cram up, nor can I say I was privileged to conceiving the use of the tactic, nor the planning of its implementation,

I was able to hear the entire roll-out of what a cram up was during the trial, complete with midnight calls and consultants who were lawyers offering up expert cram up weapons for $500,000 payments. Fortunately for my group the press was positive and everyone I dealt with was really fantastic.

In the end the Hagan Capital Group and associated funds lost the bid for American Apparel. Judge Shannon was a very capable and intelligent jurist, and it was an honor to be in his courtroom. I never reckoned that a refiling was in the cards, but it happened. In fact I had never had any experience on a Chapter 22. In case you are curious, when a company files for bankruptcy protection under Chapter 11 for a second time, it is called a Chapter 22. If a company files for Chapter 11 protection a third time it would be referred to as Chapter 33.

> This study finds that about 15% of all debtors, who emerge as continuing entities from reorganization under Chapter 11 bankruptcy, or are acquired as part of the bankruptcy process, ultimately file for bankruptcy protection again. This recidivism rate spikes to 18.25% when considering only those firms which emerge as a continuing, independent entity. This highlights what appears to be a significant recidivism problem of our Chapter 11 system.—Edward I. Altman, NYU Stern[3]

After the second bankruptcy filing (Chapter 22) American Apparel was bought by Gildan for significantly less than our bids. My group did not take part in the opportunity for the second bankruptcy, but it was very nice to read about it this time around. Oddly enough, Monarch Capital, the hedge fund holding most of the debt was at one point backed by Arlon, Conti-Grain's private equity unit. The latter joined as an investor to help Monarch regain ownership of their ownership structure. American Apparel lives on by virtue of Gildan Activewear, Inc. Gildan purchased American Apparel in bankruptcy auction for $80M. This was well below the bids we attempted but after a few years in bankruptcy, times change. It was a race to the bottom.

---

[3]Edward I. Altman, "Revisiting the Recidivism-Chapter 22 Phenomenon in the U.S. Bankruptcy System".

From a visual art and advertising perspective American Apparel stands apart. I do not know of a US clothing brand in the modern era aside from Polo by Ralph Lauren that was more successful in unifying a generation in their image of fashion. To be able to blanket their fashion ethos across the bodies of young men and women in basic apparels, while having them buy into the culture and awareness simultaneously built a brand image along with a few items of basic clothing (hoodie, V-neck, tube socks) that will be recognizable for life to a few generations is a big accomplishment. American Apparel has a tremendous back catalog of ads, many created by Dov. They were created within the vein of street art and street style, and Dov utilized the burgeoning commercialization of the style senses, both to capture a feeling in his photographic expression and to craft an easier identifier of culture in the company. While some of the ads were considered explicit, his aesthetic was vintage Los Angeles, in conjunction with commercialized street styles. The brand is still popular to this day, and though I cannot say I keep up with the company I do notice ads as I travel among major cities.

Interview with Rebecca Gooch, PhD. Campden Research

Do you foresee further integration of philanthropies and foundations in family offices or is this a special interest for family offices (like athletics, wine, art collecting)?

We have seen an increase, particularly over the last several years, in family offices being used as vehicles for philanthropic giving. When we surveyed family offices for the 2019 Global Family Office Report, we found that roughly 70% fell into this category; a figure that was proportionally up two years in a row.

However, this figure needs to be taken into context. The family office landscape is growing rapidly alongside the influx of new wealth being created, particularly in countries like the United States, China and India. In 2019, Campden Wealth Research estimated that there are roughly 7,300 single family offices worldwide, up 38% from the 5,300 estimate in 2017. Our research suggests that over two-thirds, 68%, of family offices globally were established in 2000 or later, with over half of these being established just within the last decade.

I believe that the cohort of new wealth holders can be more reliant on family offices to undertake their philanthropic giving than long-standing, multi-generational wealth holders who, in addition to having family offices, frequently have well established family foundations which oversee their philanthropic giving. In turn, it may be that the overall proportion of family offices globally that are involved in philanthropy may continue to rise alongside the growth of the family office space.

In ten years' time do you see "Impact Investing" and philanthropy joining forces as "funders" or do you see "Impact Investing" as a defined asset class subset like ESG? - *I ask because of the growing observation of impact investments being apart from financial returns and the obvious FOs interest in the field.*

In ten years' time, I believe that impact investing will stand alone as a defined asset class subset. Whilst, I believe that some family foundations will take an interest in engaging with the impact investing space due to its rising popularity, ultimately, I see impact investing and philanthropy as separate entities.

Family offices' interest in impact investing is growing at a rapid rate, with 25% now engaging in impact investing and 34% engaging more broadly in sustainable investing. Amongst these investors, impact now accounts for 14% of their average portfolio, with expectations for this to rise to 25% by 2024. Furthermore, in 2019, over three-fifths of family offices globally reported to believe that the majority of their peers will invest sustainably by 2022.

What is, in part, driving this growth is that the impact investing space is maturing and becoming increasingly profitable. In fact, 81% of family offices' impact investments met or exceeded expectations in 2019 when compared to traditional investments.

Another important factor to consider is that we are in the early stages of a significant generational transition. We know that the next generation, and millennials in particular, are a powerful force which is driving the rise in impact investing. In turn, the next 10 years will be an important period to watch, as a significant portion of Next Gens (37%) are expected to take the reins and oversee their family wealth. Over a quarter (28%) reportedly already have, and I believe that this is a key factor with regard to how far impact investing has already come to date.

In ten years' time do you see a well-defined regulation and oversight framework of family offices globally? - *I ask because there is little oversight in the countries I operate in (United States and England).*

[I am not an expert on family office regulation, so I cannot give you an in-depth opinion here. I can only say the following…]

I do not envision the regulatory landscape changing substantially over the next 10 years in well-established family office jurisdiction, such as the United States and Europe. In the United States, for example, holistically speaking, the Trump administration has been more focused on deregulation than greater regulation. However, all of this could change in the 2020 elections if, for example, Elizabeth Warren gets elected. Her stance towards UHNWs will likely be very different to Donald Trump's. In such a case, the political winds can change significantly.

Outside of these two regions, we can also see an emergence of new wealth in Asia-Pacific, alongside a growth in the number of family offices there. Many areas do not yet have regulatory systems that are specifically applicable to family offices there. In turn, over the coming decade, some new regulatory frameworks may emerge. However, a number of these areas, such as Singapore, are looking to attract families of wealth and their family offices, so they may look at ways of incentivising wealth holders to set-up there.

What are the main challenges ahead for global family offices from your point of view?

The family office space will face a variety of challenges in the coming years. The first stems from the natural evolution of the space. At present, the number of new family offices in existence is growing rapidly. Certain jurisdictions are better equipped to set up and operate in than others. For instance, if a family is located in London or New York, it will have access to a plethora of top advisors, professional staff and promising investment opportunities. However, if it is based in an area where family offices and financial services are less developed, such as certain parts of India or China, it may face set-up, operational and investment challenges. This is all part of the natural growing pains and maturity of the sector.

Another factor to consider is where the global economy is headed. In 2019, 55% of family offices reported to believe that we will enter a recession by 2020. In preparation for a potential economic downturn, 45% of family offices realigned their investment strategies and 42% increased their cash reserves. Given that we are in the late stages of a lengthy economic cycle, market conditions may again be an obstacle that family offices must face.

In addition to these challenges, family offices will have to adapt to rapidly evolving technology. At present, nine-in-10 family offices reportedly believe that artificial intelligence will be the next biggest disruptive force in global business. Another 57% believe that blockchain technology will fundamentally change the way we invest in the future. If family offices do not adapt to, and in many cases (Fig. 6.1).

How Do Family Offices Invest?

Families invest differently. A well-managed family-owned enterprise increases the family fortune as the business value increases, as most family businesses are owned by the operators. Studies have shown that family businesses benefit from the family shareholders having a stake in the company—and an understanding of how the wealth was derived—and enterprises controlled by family members have a chance of lasting longer than other companies. From this, historical patterns prevail in modern times. A hardworking entrepreneur or a second-generation family-owned business leader takes the initiative to carve out industry for themselves.

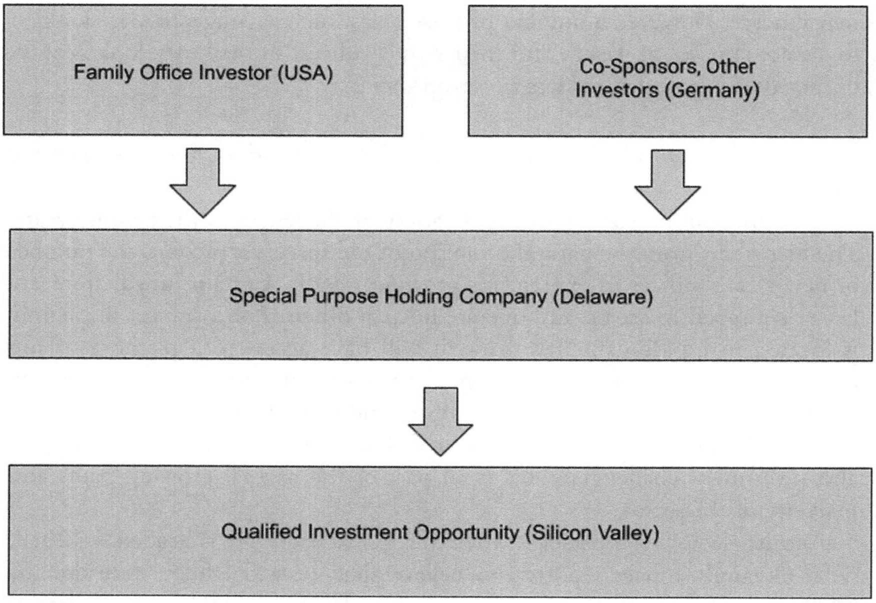

Fig. 6.1 Direct investment structure

One of the great American family fortunes—Mars, Inc.—was created in part by a father (Franklin Clarence Mars) and son (Forrest Edward Mars Sr.) who rarely spoke to one another, and throughout their careers they remained in the same industry, with son Forrest taking over the reins of Mars, Inc. once Franklin passed away. They reunited later in life but it is American-style temerity where you have prevailing interests and interfamily ascendancy, despite seemingly counterintuitive communication and dysfunction looming overhead like any typical family drama.

FOs are highly customized to the needs of the family. This may be separate from the business operations or this may overlap within the business operations. Most FOs maintain a healthy balance from a management perspective but that is not always the case. A commonality I find in North American family offices—and family-run businesses—is that families can remain over-invested in a certain segment or niche and at times seem obsessed within that particular industry. For instance, Canada and Texas are both heavy in natural resources and commodities, it is not a stretch for investors and families who have made money in those industries to stay invested in that industry for life or multiple generations—long after the original business was sold off. While this is not a cause for alarm, it is definitely a call to arms and families should take to study the entire supply chain of such industries, and factor in all risks and study healthy asset diversification. Family offices are by nature long-term investors but the most ardent of investors cannot overcome the destruction of certain types of employment like telephone switchboard operators or marchands de coquilles d'escargots (Paris snail shell collectors who scooped up customer shells from waste bins and resold them to kitchens).

Family names in money management and investment are common, from Jack Bogle and his son John, to legions of generations of financiers from American capital cities such as George Herbert Walker Bush's grandfather and namesake, George Herbert Walker who founded the American investment banker G. H. Walker & Co., which was later bought by the Boston Brahmin led firm of White, Weld & Co. and then later absorbed in Merrill Lynch. A more relevant example of a family office acting as investors and financial groups think of Sid Bass and his brother Robert Bass. Both became well-known investors and philanthropists and both were sons of Perry Richardson Bass of the Texas oil fortune. Perry was a business partner of his uncle Sid Richardson. Despite the family connections and the passing of wealth from one generation to another, families are prone to invest differently and at times one family office spawns many single family offices, all who direct their wealth and devote their fortunes to their own reality with a strike of independence.

Direct Investing over Traditional Private Equity

North American banks are now all too familiar with the idea of tapping a family or family's pool of capital to enable a strategic opportunity, but this hasn't always been the case. Direct investing is perhaps the secret to family longevity. The pivot from passive investing to active investing from a family perspective is incredibly lucrative. The family can systematically organize shareholders and family members as executive, or at the very least advisory board members or actual professionals with the enterprise.

Beginning in 1956, the A. C. Israel family began to invest in direct private equity opportunities when they purchased 11 drugstores in Ohio. The drugstores merged with the NYSE traded Peoples Drugstores Inc. in 1976. I have no idea the fortune made in this transaction but I am sure it was sizable.

Investing in third party private equity management is becoming less and less attractive to families. The model is not broken but in need of heavy retooling like the hedge fund world. It has been unfairly tiered and at times highly opaque. For a time some of the wealthier families in America—just not the wealthiest—were unable to invest in private equity. If they did have the chance it was often very far down the line in the capital calls, perhaps as the lasting and the last out. The reality is Carlyle Group tapping a family for a seven- to ten-year $500M investment is not applicable to most family offices and family investment groups. Equally as unpalatable is investing as a minority investor and risking dilution and having virtually no say in any part of the enterprise. There is often no value add apart from the opportunity to invest. Investors are also tired of being sidelined for the investment funds either by design or by lack of opportunity. It is important to note that on May 04, 2019 Warren Buffet and Charlie Munger—at their annual meeting in Omaha—warned, heavily against private equity funds, going as far as to accuse them of lying about their returns to better position themselves in the fundraising race.

In the last decade families participating in direct investments have been an ever increasing reality and brokerage houses have been at odds with changing demographics. Co-investing, either through a joint venture or through a third-party managed relationship has also become quite common. Co-investing by nature align interests and create partnerships that often last well into the future. After all, it makes plenty of sense for a middle market packaging business owned by a family to buy a forest from another family, or to coinvest with another entity either family-owned or independent, using family finance or capital markets finance. I believe the model has been broken for a very long time and because of a faulty model and the continued disconnect investors have grown wiser over generations. After all, it pays to do your own research and it is hardly fashionable to be an unsustainable and dysfunctional in finance, let alone life. Despite the model being broken there is little to match the world of investing—particularly in America—and investors continue to show up to the table no matter the generation, gender, or ethnic background.

Today fintech trading firms offer free equity trades to the general public but this is a very recent development. Another clear issue is that investors have been actively investing for decades and investment banks have unfairly placed them into specific categories, separated by net worth and revenue. Different categories have different opportunities to invest in different investments, to a degree. The clients who make the bank the most money receive the best investments to invest in. To a degree the investment system has been slanted to one side—the side that makes the bank money—and unless you are part of that team you are generally left out of the mix. However, that world is now more and more dominated by institutional trading houses, their trading systems, and market makers who are often the same players in the risk on risk off world of stock markets. Moreover, investors of means have sat on the sidelines for far too long witnessing IPO's pop and make investors seemingly easy millions while most everyone—from main street investor or multimillionaire wary of investment houses, long-promised riches through cheap trading fees—had to deal with the shorter end of the stick. This still goes on, but now FOs are part of the equation. In many ways family office investors now must educate themselves and they must educate their family otherwise they stand to fall victim to the heartless machine of the investment world, but the upside could double or triple existing fortunes.

In the early part of the last century the world of commodity and stock market investing in the United State has been all but efficient and widely fractured, cumbersome, and confusing. In 1975 the Securities and Exchange Commission allowed brokerage houses to negotiate rates and out came a new type of stockbroker: the discount brokerage. Still, investors had a tremendous amount of trouble accessing research and market data with necessary transparency for decades and decades. The futures and commodity markets were the first to jump into technological innovation as early as the 1970s but it took a few more decades for American equity markets to catch on. The mild American recession in 1990, which lasted a mere eight months, led to nonstop growth—arguably accelerated by the 1996 Telecommunications Act and the 1997 Taxpayer Relief Act—that only sputtered because of the dotcom bubble. The 1990s differed from the 1980s in many parts but first and foremost the difference was the 1990s was an area of shrinking budgets and surpluses and growing payrolls. NBER estimates that the US stock market capitalization value doubled between 1990 and 1995 and then tripled between 1995 and 2000.[4]

The greed of the 1980s, the year-over-year payroll growth of the 1990s, the dotcom bubble, and the Great Recession have left an unprecedented mark on American financial legacies. This last time it was not only equities but asset-backed securities which were constructed to look, act, and feel like bonds, complete with the security of a bond. Their only drawback was if the portfolio manager happened to buy debt which defaulted, and many did and are doing so again and again. It is no different than the 1980s and 1990s when brokers and the wirehouses controlled the information flow and pushed securities on unassuming retail investors. The end goal for this type was and still is to bring in new money.

Family offices tend to move faster if they are investing directly, even more if they are investing directly into their core industry. Most FOs have a core

[4]NBER Working Paper Series, "The Dot-Com Bubble, Bush Deficits and the US Current Account" Working Paper 11543, p. 3.

industry or were built around a core industry and still hold that element of expertise. It is not assured but widely accepted that while family offices focus on diversifying, they also focus on refining score attributes. I will go into greater detail on this practice in later chapters. I spoke with a friend and associate Marc Baine about SFOs and their increasing activity in capital markets, including taking on middle market and bulge bracket deals. Marc and I had worked together on many projects and he has witnessed family offices—especially the very large FOs—taking a much more active approach in the world of syndicated PE and buyouts. Baine, a financier in Manhattan and a former Goldman Sachs banker observed a tremendous amount of market activity as well as working directly with numerous single family offices:

> Over the last three years covering Single Family Offices from the institutional side is that the migration to a more professionalized process of sourcing deal flow, trading, governance, ideas you name it. Many Family Offices are hiring Wall Street, Private Equity professionals as the increasingly the level of sophistication has gone up. In 2017 that there were roughly 10,000 Family Offices globally and the U.S. has an estimated 3,000 with $1.2T in assets plus half were set up in the last 15 years. So, as you can see that over the next 20 plus years the Family Office Community will continue to grow given the wealth transfer that will be taking place and the family's desire for more control of their assets in directing capital. Family Offices control $4T in assets and hedge funds & private equity control roughly $5.7T in assets. They've been buying distressed debt, real estate and esoteric insurance products. The offices proliferate partly because of a surge in global wealth in recent decades, traceable in part to high levels of merger activity and IPOs. The number of billionaires in the world rose 6.4% in 2015 to a record 2,473. It says their collective wealth reached nearly $7.7 trillion. Given the shift of Family Offices waiting to have more and more control of the investment decisions, I predict the trend of Family Offices doing more direct deal flow and less allocation to hedge funds and private equity. Also, almost a third of the Family Offices they surveyed are engaged in impact investing. Majority of those driving the focus on impact investing within the family offices are the next generation of families. With the public equity markets many might say is overvalued and fixed income yielding next to nothing, I've experienced time and time again Family Offices desiring to hunt for private deals amongst themselves. The billionaire Pritzker family out of Chicago raised $1.8B from wealthy families for a fund (PPC Partners) targeting middle market, family/entrepreneur owned companies (sectors like packaging and healthcare industries). "We wanted to form a bit of a club, in that we wanted to gather a select group of people who thought about investing the way we did, were supportive of how we invested" so says Paul Carbone co-head of PPC Partners. What's unique about the Pritzker's setup is that the fund is blurring the lines between private equity and family offices. Family Offices

usually have a much longer investment time horizon (10 plus years) than say private equity firms (5-7 years), so many times they will have a "leg up" as we say in getting a family run business to partner with them given their history with the Hyatt Hotels and The Marmon Group (which has since been sold to Berkshire Hathaway).[5]

The mainstream adaptation of real-time applications (apps) and fully connected data visualized dashboards has leveled the playing field but only after the intensity of the situation hit an all-time high. The new generation of investors inside parts of Generation X, the Millennials, and Generation Z see the world in a different light and for that the industry—meaning the institutional finance industry—has come 360 degrees. The amateur investor has never had a better opportunity, a growing trend in the United States and North America a growing trend over the last century has been for well-to-do families to take a more active role in the management of assets and wealth. This may represent a cultural shift in response to a growing negative sentiment to big business finance, partially for reasons I mentioned in the previous paragraphs. This could also be basic Darwinism at play or it could be a combination of both: those who created the fortune can often train and manage better than others so they might as well have a say in the finances. This could also be the common-sense notion of wealth being developed over multiple generations, with each generation passing on some elements of management and trade—if not an entire play book. Developments in financial technology and communication have only leveled the playing field and increased the sophistication of management and abilities for amateurs to become professionals and for families to involve their children in the active management of the enterprise, which has been shown to increase the over stability and longevity of the enterprise. Families can empower themselves to protect their capital verse handing it over to a smooth talking wealth manager who needs to increase his revenue to pay his jet fuel fees. As I will discuss throughout this book, FOs have a sense of urgency and they have a sense of reserve. They are all similar in the fact that they are unique different—apart from sharing social-economic behaviors—and that they have permanent capital. Apart from that it is impossible to say if FOs are slow or fast, risky or reserved (Fig. 6.2).

Private Equity denotes shareholder equity in private companies through private ownership or fund ownership. Real Estate covers REITS, CRE, and Luxury Residential (Non-Primary) Dwellings.

---

[5]Marc Baine, The Baine Companies.

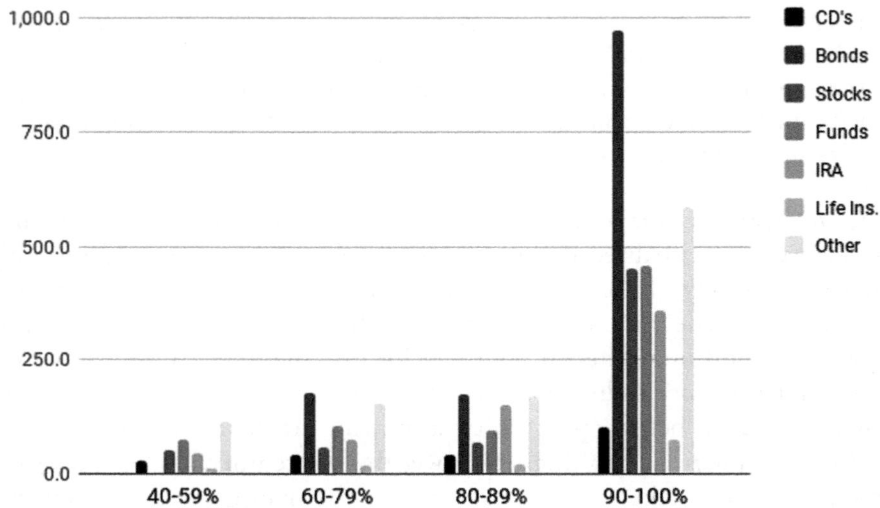

Fig. 6.2 The United States—Top 50% allocations (as of 2019)

Allocations

As can be expected, family offices driven by the entrepreneurial force who created the wealth often choose to stay invested in those particular industries. At times these risks reap sizable rewards; entrepreneurs can have special knowledge in industries from experience and equal experience in risk-taking which can lead to detailed intelligence, which serves as an edge against competition, but clearly this it is not always guaranteed. Notice in the givenchart venture capital, private equity, and hedge fund (hedge funds and derivatives of such are included in alternatives) allocations are quite small. While debated I support the view the venture capital is an asset class and investments in venture capital should be limited to small percentages of an investor's aggregate net worth, unless the investor is active in such industry or unless the investor is active in the venture capital industry. VC is one of the best ways to lose a fortune barring financing speculative Hollywood movies. As mentioned earlier traditional private equity does not always align with FO's interests. The same can be said for market trading and financial instruments. As for the hedge fund world in recent years this has been dismantled and sadly there is not much of a story behind it; with market fundamentals separating from true fundamentals and trampling over an explosion of data—combined with high fees and high risk without the returns—investors have been withdrawing funds. Many of these small investors have taking trading on themselves. The FOs subset is no different. If a family office has the appetite and knowledge to trade, many do. It is worth noting that exposure to hedge funds from the FOs' side has shrunk dramatically when compared to the 1980s or 1990s. For the families that remain active many have internalized their own funds to give children jobs and watch over the risky investments chasing constant oversized returns. Many modern hedge fund barons are also technology entrepreneurs and have been able to pass along trading systems and deep. The world of hedge funds, alternative funds, and venture capital funds often has a certain family office patina but while the wealthy historically have had hands in these types of investments, it is not a rule that is followed with any regularity.

Family offices take many routes to investment: return on investment or internal rate of return and so forth. These are worthwhile terms to utilize but they are by no means the standard. There is not a status quo for allocations in the world of family offices and this for a number of reasons, the most common reason being the family is well-to-do and can afford to ignore the status quo. When a family is wealthy the principal concentration of wealth can and will change. By nature allocations and outlooks on those assets will change and planning and providing for the family may take center stage. Perhaps the creator wishes to provide education and capital for business, careers, and housing for a vast extended clan of 200–300 family members. That setup and execution plan will undoubtedly different from a family legacy centered around one family foundation

In most wealthy families trusts, foundations and careful estate planning are par for the course. When politicians rant and rave on television about inheritance tax it often falls on deaf ears. A reason could be that there is a loyal industry filled with experienced people ready to advise and design plans to help anyone with a few hundred thousand in investable assets, let alone millions or billions. Planning around inheritance tax and avoiding probate and any unnecessary estate taxes are common discussed topics in America. In Chapter 8 I delve into trusts and foundations.

Bibliography

See Continental Grain (CGC) Corporate History, www.continentalgrain.com/culture/heritage/.

See Bunge Corporation (New York) v Tradax Export SA (Panama) [1981] UKHL 11 (25 February 1981).

Edward I. Altman, "Revisiting the Recidivism-Chapter 22 Phenomenon in the U.S. Bankruptcy System".

See page 3, NBER Working Paper Series, "The Dot-Com Bubble, Bush Deficits and the US Current Account" Working Paper 11543, p. 3.

From Marc Baine, The Baine Companies, New York City, New York. Marc is a Goldman Sachs alumnus and investment banker.

7

Governance, Succession, and Fraud

The inner workings of family offices are unique. However, families often display similarities and much can be said about family offices. In most instances, family offices provide employment and income for heirs and stakeholders and in most instances, those stakeholders are given positions according to their skillset and qualifications. In other situations, family offices act as independent advisory comprised of financiers

Governance, Costs Associated, Employment, Workforce Characteristics & Executives

Requirements to lead a family office vary. If you are a UHNW and HNWI, the costs associated with opening an SFO are quite low in America, when compared to the costs to pay specialists from attorneys, to trustees, financiers, and brokers. Most single family offices are small, and many include full-time and part-time employees; from legal advisors, to in-house counsel, in-house advisors and economists, and in-house accounting. As stated earlier, many SFOs begin inside existing business offices, and then as transitions or events happen, staff stay on and take over SFO matters. Apart from the above, associated costs are hard to gauge from a standard perspective. If a family owns private aircraft and yachts, they probably need to add charter service employees or start a chartering arm for efficiency. I often find the SFOs realize savings from starting a family office as one is cutting ties with other business

C. Hagan, *Global Family Office Investing*,
https://doi.org/10.1007/978-3-030-18224-3_7

service providers and adding these services in-house like legal and accounting. Some SFOs decide to bring everything inside the house.

If a family office were to begin as a reporting and advisory unit, the initial staff could be quite streamlined. Apart from analysts and researchers with financial experience, the staff could exist with as few as a handful of employees.

Employment in the two industries is a mixed bag, with asset management leading to longer employment terms that last well over a decade, and administration having a higher turnover. A commonality among senior partners working in family offices is the opportunity to invest or become invested in various funds, portfolio companies, and investments. I do not agree that family office staff and payroll should be based on AUM, but the model persists on FOs seeking top talent. If the family office is to be an active investor in sophisticated financial products in the capital markets, the family office would need a confident bench of talent. For instance, if a family office were to run internal investment strategies, a portfolio manager would be needed. If there were multiple strategies perhaps multiple managers are needed. Portfolio managers command a high salary, and top portfolio managers command some of the highest salaries in the world, let alone commissions and equity ownership.

Family Office Employee Matrix:

(1) Executives: Chairman, CEO, COO, CFO or managing partner, and managing directors;
(2) Management Operations: Portfolio Managers, Risk Managers,
(3) General Office Staff: Accounting, Huma Resources, Office Assistants;
(4) Direct Investing: Analysts, traders, and banking relationship managers.

Key employees in Manhattan for a billionaire who is an active securities trader; yachtsman and helicopter pilot, will likely trend toward a higher income. Maybe the family office wants to send a message to the world and pay as much as bulge bracket banks do and compete for top talent. In contrast, a fifth-generation family office in Savannah, Georgia that only manages investment grade credit may pay well below market rates for talent and staff for a number of reasons but primarily geography. Another difference is the shareholder stakeholder matrix. If some of the shareholders are managers or executives, compensation is going to largely lie in the shares and dividends from securities ownership.

A family office and for that matter any form of family office management should attempt to vertically integrate as much as they can. By bringing a high percentage of such services in-house (at times 90%) outside service providers are consulted with less regularity. Executive office payroll, certified audits, and legal expenses are among the highest expenses FOs experience. Research is an expense now with MiFID II and so is associated travel and banking. Family offices often loan money to family members in the form of mortgages or debt finance, which can in turn put internal capital to work if properly allocated and well-managed from a credit standpoint.

Apart from succession and ownership, governance of the family office depends on how the family establishes the FO. Often family offices employ family members and family members may choose to employ assistants or managers to handle their responsibilities. Often family members are active professionals in the associated industries therefore directly oversee the managed assets or have an active stake in the future of the enterprise. When family members are not commercially inclined or opt not to work, the situation often becomes one of the passive stakeholder who is also an inheritor.

Succession in the Family Office World

It is my opinion that the single most important aspect of a family office entity and a family office enterprise is the ability to decide how succession works. Change is inevitable but many struggle to accept change and when there are assets and offspring, let alone second and third marriages and second and third families, making tough decisions only become tougher. With the next generation always waiting in the wings for direction and succession, families that plan accordingly reap the benefits. Most family offices are held by stakeholders who are family members. In this situation, family members have stakes in the FO and therefore have stakes in assets contained in the FO. Vesting a family member, heir, or offspring as a stakeholder in the FO is often the first step.

A common thread found among the next generation is the change of management style, a change in the perception of risk and a willingness to modernize, even if it is purely an analytical exercise. Additionally, the leaders of the family are often the most vocal members of the family, those showing an active interest in the businesses or holding company enterprises as a whole.

As Deloitte University shared in their 2016 report on family business: our research found that the most common attribute that is considered when deciding which family member should be groomed for leadership is his/her expression of interest in becoming the next leader. Other factors that are generally considered desirable are work experience within the family business (and a good understanding of it), followed by experience gained outside the company. Experience in working for other companies increases the self-esteem and self-confidence of the next generation, and gives them wider business experience and greater credibility with non-family employees.[1]

Perhaps the most important factor in family business and family offices is this: for the next generation to successfully rise to the occasion, the next generation must first show interest and inclination.

White-Collar Crime and the FBI

I will end this chapter with an interesting story. Bad actors are in the financial world, and the family office world is no different. To some degree family offices have a bit of a target on them, as they are perceived as big piles of easy money managed without much oversight.

As one can expect, family offices receive a lot of deal flow and field a lot of requests for capital. FOs operate in a closed circle to a degree, I am no different. My inner circle is somewhat insulated from the annoyances of triviality, but still, I am not immune to receiving communications from random people looking for money and at times I receive urgent requests for funding from third parties I do not know. In almost every case, unsolicited requests are ignored, but one situation stands out prominently. Many years ago I received unsolicited offers from an entrepreneur and investor I had no ties to. He was selling his founder shares at a heavy discount and was looking to close the deal as soon as possible. This was odd for a few reasons, and upon further investigation, it revealed criminal aspects. I sent off a few emails to a state securities regulator and soon I was swapping phone calls with the state and a local journalist who was covering this story. Some of the story had slipped into the news and a few journalists were bouncing the facts back and forth and working on a story. I realized that I had gained the trust of the fraudster so I decided I would keep it working and share my findings with the journalists.

I kept in touch with the fraudster and asked him for more information on the investment. I was given access to the company data room. Then, I was put in contact with the FBI by my state securities office contact.

The FBI agent was very intelligent. We spoke at length about investment fraud and the agent shared the criminal's backstory with me, which was word

[1] Next-generation family businesses, Deloitte University.

for word accurate to the story I had heard from the journalists and state regulators. There was no way around it; this guy was a serious fraudster and a serious menace to innocent American investors.

If you have ever wondered how quickly criminal cases escalate, this case was a lesson in stealth operations. Literally within a few weeks of discovering the fraud, I was working on a step-by-step plan with the agency to get the founder on tape, lying about his revenues, bogus sales and billionaire investors. I still have the notes from the sting operation. Unfortunately there were no code names or secret drop-off locations, as all of this took place over the phone and through emails like a standard investment due to diligence review. It was quite nerve wracking but definitely exciting.

I developed a rapport with the special agent and became comfortable talking with him about the fraud at hand and just how bad it was. At one point I asked the special agent if he thought I would be in any danger. The agent reminded me the fraudster was running a scam because he was, after all, very desperate for money and probably not dangerous, which was somewhat reassuring.

I had yet to review the data room. I had logged in a few times just in case the fraudster was paying attention to my user activity, but I hadn't taken the time to review the documents.

The fraudster was lying about every nuance of his business and had put forth a tremendous scam involving fake numbers, fake investors, fake signatures on investment documents, and shambolic numbers showing an unstoppable meteoric rise.

After about a week of review, I called the fraudster on a taped line. I called him maybe three times. Each call we went over line items in the budget, line items on the slide deck, and financials from the data room. Over and over again I led him down the path of no return, listening to him lie about generating tens of millions in revenue per year and sharing his illustrious list of blue-chip clientele over and over again.

Being around all of this crime started to bother me and I became irritated that I was caught up in such a fiasco with the fraudster. I began to heavily resent him and I wanted him in jail. I was blown away by his propensity to deceive and his belief that investors had endless supplies of money. For a moment I thought about investing just so I could press charges against him myself and see him put in jail. I had reached a breaking point.

Fortunately the FBI gave me free reign to lead the fraudster on. Each time I spoke with him, I would turn on the recorder and go down the path, having him repeat everything he had said previously, all the situations, all the one-liners, all the flash in the pan deception stories I had become accustomed to during this short relationship. To my benefit, the crook rarely veered from his story. He literally repeated himself word for word, each time on tape.

Eventually the sting was over. I had done my duty. While helping the FBI take down a criminal may sound a bit overwhelming, it felt very good to do my part to take down a bad guy. I am very grateful for the FBI's assistance. Despite the thrill of adventure, the case was exhausting. I will never forget the feeling I felt when I finally comprehended the level of deception that was going on. Ultimately, I believe he stole over $50M dollars from investors.

Bibliography

Next-generation Family Business, Deloitte University.

8

Philanthropy

A very good example of a trust still in existence in American can be found both in the Hearst family of California and the Campbell family of Hawaii (Figs. 8.1 and 8.2). The trusts were created to hold and manage assets for a large number of descendants. Both enlisted trusts to extend the life of the enterprise and to keep control in the family. The Hearst trust is still in existence and pays out dividends to some sixty-plus family members. The founder of the family, George Hearst was born in 1820 and was a millionaire from speculative mining by the 1850s. To this day the company remains private, is located in the Hearst Tower in Manhattan, and in 2016 had revenues over $10B. As of printing the chairman of the board is William Randolph Hearst III. His namesake, William Randolph Hearst stipulated that the trust be dissolved upon the last death of his then living grandchild. Hearst the elder was convinced his sons were unfit to lead his empire, and left the power and control to managers, who were responsible to the board. The board contains a set number of seats, occupied by a minority stake held by family members. The empire is run by non-family members, and branches of the family hold seats as trustees, with a non-family member majority of trustees. It is unique in the sense that it preserves the holdings, but keeps the family from obtaining total control and taking over the Heart enterprise. It is also unique in the sense that the empire has grown significantly and undoubtedly still with the help of William Randolph Hearst's grand vision. Today the Hearst family is valued at around $30 billion.

C. Hagan, *Global Family Office Investing*,
https://doi.org/10.1007/978-3-030-18224-3_8

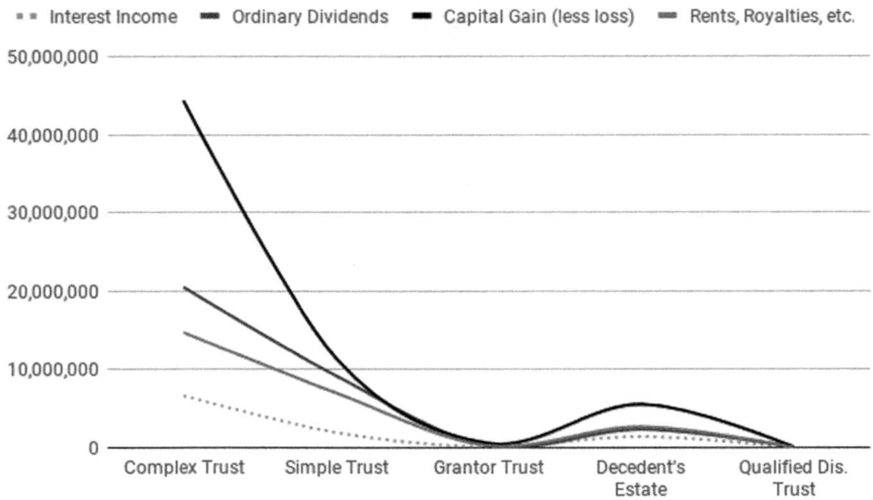

Fig. 8.1 Taxation of trust funds

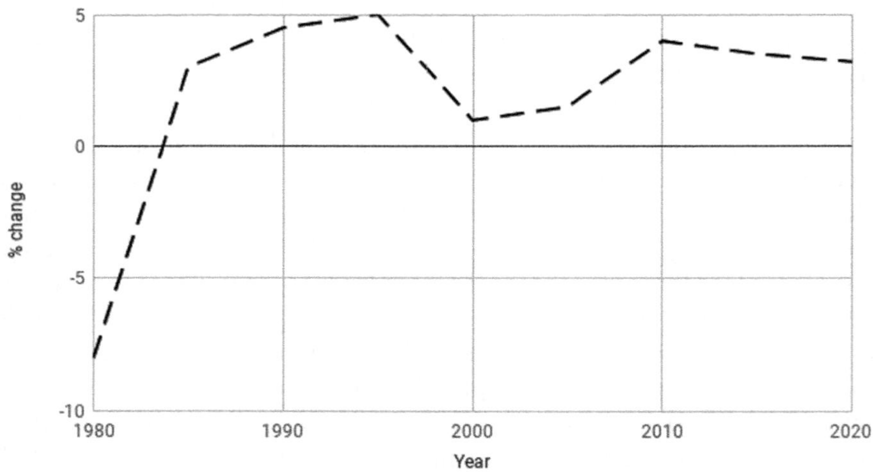

Fig. 8.2 US GDP Real Growth (Pre-Covid)

James Campbell was just 13 years old when he left his home in Londonderry, Ireland, stowing away on a ship to seek his fortune in the New World. He eventually found his way to the Pacific, arriving in Hawai'i in 1850 at the age of 24. Here he began a brilliant business career that spanned 50 years, starting as a carpenter, then a sugar mill owner, eventually becoming one of Hawaii's largest landowners, with holdings on O'ahu, Maui and the Island of Hawai'i. These holdings formed the basis of his wealth. When he died in 1900, Campbell's will directed that his estate, valued at $3 million, be held

> in trust for the benefit of his wife, Abigail Kuaihelani Maipinepine, his four daughters and their offspring. Under the terms of the will, the trust terminated on January 20, 2007 following the death of his last surviving daughter. That same year, the majority of the heirs of the Estate of James Campbell elected to receive their distribution as shares in the newly formed James Campbell Company.[1]

Joseph Campbell is another grand example of century-centric management. Now headquartered in Kapolei, Hawaii and San Francisco, California, the Joseph Campbell holdings were in a trust which was dissolved after one hundred and seven years and the holdings were reorganized into a company called the James Campbell Company. It in turn became one of Hawaii's largest companies. With over thirty heirs, all but three heirs stayed in the company, meaning three took buyouts of some sort. The remainder of the heirs took shares in the new venture. The transition and conversion plan began in 1988 and ended in 2007 with the formation of the aforementioned company. No small task by any step and likely handled with very few outsiders. The company is growing and making acquisitions while remaining private and focused on core business activities.

An Irrevocable Life Insurance Trust, often called an ILIT, is a common family office and estate planning tool. This is standard use in the FOs world, from SFO to MFO. It is very common for well-to-do families and individuals to use life insurance and trusts in unison. It is very common for well-to-do families to set up special needs trusts for family members or loved ones in dispose of. ILITs are used to avoid probate and provide for tax efficiency. They are also used to fund other trust funds for heirs and dependents, and to pay capital gains taxes on asset sales, and to pay for tax burdens from asset sales. An ILIT is a very versatile and effective estate planning vehicle.

Commercial trustees and trusts in North America have been in use for a very long time. Their base is UK common law, which is centered on equity and equitable settlement. Trust companies and commercial trustees (banks or trust companies) have been at the core of multi-generational wealth management in America for a century or more. As mentioned early, a trust and the agreement often used in a trust—the indenture—in the cases of Hearst and Duke legacies have succeeded at implementing their fortunes into society, thereby being engraved in the minds of many the illustriousness of the family and the families fortune through the actions of science, education, and civic unity.

---

[1] Statement from the James Campbell Company LLC.

Trusts focused on distributing all the trusts funds to charities, also known as charitable trusts, are also very common. Part of the Astor family fortune ended up in a charitable trust and many American families have left millions and millions in charitable trusts to be managed like a foundation while jointly distributing principle in the form of grants and salaries to managers of the trust, business associates and associate family members.

Trusts were once a dominant force in estate planning and inheritance but now they have competition. I have mentioned trusts a number of times in this book primarily due to their presence in history—they've been used to pass the ownership of wealth to other heirs for hundreds of years in American and are still used in many forms from life insurance trusts to special trusts holding complex rights and licenses.

Trusts are quite common but they are also cumbersome, costly, and complicated. An attractive structure in a single family office is the fact that trusts can hold assets, as well as easily managed by the trustees who can be housed in the family office.

Trusts

One of the tricks of the trade is to establish a trust in an offshore jurisdiction that benefits a company based in another jurisdiction, and to establish the trustee in a neutral country or perhaps a country with very strong trust and banking privacy laws. While this book is not a book about trusts, it is a book covering the practice of family office and trusts are a part of planning and succession. Moreover, families deriving wealth from regulated holdings like broadcast media, sports teams, and royalties are known to use trusts to avoid conflicts of interest. This is very similar to the pattern Rockefeller and Morgan used in the days before antitrust laws to enhance their fortunes, thus lending the word to the phrase "trust busting." Rockefeller and Morgan had created a system of interlocking trusts, which cross owned assets, jointly and separately, thereby creating a once in a lifetime solid system of influence and market control, also known as a monopoly. Still, trusts are used to this day to hold assets for future generations if for nothing else for its murky history.

Families and entities may choose to become a state or nationally chartered trust. Nevada is one state which has chosen to loosen the laws around trust companies. Below are the minimum equity requirements required to establish and operate a trust company in the state of Nevada, as well as the abbreviated laws and regulation for a family trust company:

NRS 669.100 Minimum stockholders' equity required for organization and operation.

1. No retail trust company may be organized or operated with a stockholders' equity of less than $1,000,000, or in such greater amount as may be required by the Commissioner.
2. A retail trust company shall maintain at least 25 percent of its required stockholders' equity in cash and at least an additional 25 percent of its required stockholders' equity in cash or cash equivalents comprising certificates of deposit, money market funds or other insured deposits.
3. Any grandfathered trust company other than a noncustodial trust company that does not have the minimum capital required by this section as of October 1, 2009, shall:
   (a) Except as otherwise determined by the Commissioner, increase its capital to a minimum of:
   (1) By October 1, 2010, $500,000;
   (2) By October 1, 2011, $750,000; and
   (3) By October 1, 2012, $1,000,000; and
4. Any noncustodial trust company that does not have the minimum capital required by this section as of October 1, 2009, shall:
   (a) Except as otherwise determined by the Commissioner, increase its capital to a minimum of:
      (1) By October 1, 2010, $350,000;
      (2) By October 1, 2011, $400,000; and
      (3) By October 1, 2012, $500,000; and

NRS 669.042 "Family trust company" defined.

1. "Family trust company" means a corporation or limited-*liability company that:*
   (a) Acts or proposes to act as a fiduciary;
   (b) Is organized or qualified to do business in this State to serve family members;

South Dakota Family Trust

South Dakota has established a private trust program for families and businesses. Over the past five years, assets under management and in custody have swelled in South Dakota. Having seen these types of programs before in the United States, I have noticed in the marketplace and in private research that the South Dakota Private Trust is being utilized by sophisticated multi-state families and it is being used in international systems for international family offices.

> Private trust company defined. A private trust company is one that does not engage in trust company business with the general public or otherwise hold itself out as a trustee or fiduciary for hire by advertising, solicitation, or other means and instead operates for the benefit of a family or families, regardless of whether compensation is received or anticipated. Private trust companies limit activities to the management of private assets, usually for the benefit of a single family lineage.[2]

Additionally, South Dakota is a stable state, and one that is willing to try new products and regulations. Trusts are not subject to gift, estate, inheritance, or income taxes. The state also allows for the trust of unlimited durations.

Trust Companies

If a family has a large family and needs to plan for a large number of descendants, establishing a state chartered trust company is a good idea and a worthwhile plan of action to unify the family. A family as large and well-to-do as Cargill can easily handle such. Rockefeller has long had a trust company. The state of Nevada has the most progressive trust company laws today. The costs associated with opening a nationally charged trust company would make one open the service to others (perhaps other families). Regardless, families may elect to establish a regulated trust company. This is common for large SFOs. Fees depend on the jurisdiction, but banking fees for the Caymans and Bermuda are palatable. Most international banks with trust departments and multi-family offices have offshore trustee abilities.

Offshore Trusts

The obvious cohorts still remain the dominant players. Bermuda and the Caymans are very strong for establishing companies and chartering trusts companies and administering trusts, but so are Monaco, the Seychelles, Malta, Switzerland, and others. There is no such thing as an offshore asset protection trust as by nature trusts are used for asset protection. You can design a complex system of trusts to meet your needs and may call this an asset protection trust if so inclined. At the very best, an offshore trust is a trust that has the trustees set up in a low ta, or zero tax jurisdiction. Often they also

[2]Trust Companies, South Dakota Department of Labor & Regulation.

have jurisdictional laws to protect the trusts from creditors, assuming there is no legal wrongdoing.

Revocable Trusts

Revocable trusts are created during the lifetime of the trust creator and can be altered, changed, modified, or revoked entirely. Often called a living trust, these are trusts in which the trust creator transfers the title of a property to a trust, serves as the initial trustee, and has the ability to remove the property from the trust during his or her lifetime. Revocable trusts are extremely helpful in avoiding probate. If the ownership of assets is transferred to a revocable trust during the lifetime of the trust creator so that it is owned by the trust at the time of the trust creator's death, the assets will not be subject to probate.

Land Trust or Illinois Land Trust

Land trusts are sometimes called "Illinois-type land trusts" for historical reasons.

Trusts like these may be held by nonprofits or by corporations. In America, land trusts and conservation easements are very popular. If done correctly they are very effective, not only from income tax credits or tax breaks, but also as a tool to hold the assets in perpetual trust, for conservation.

Irrevocable Trust

An irrevocable trust is a trust that cannot be altered after it is created. Similarly, once an asset is transferred to the trust, it cannot be removed. A useful example is an ILIT, as discussed in Chapter 1.

Charitable Trust

Charitable trusts are trusts which are established to pay out to a certain charity or the public in general. Typically charitable trusts are established as part of an estate plan to lower or avoid imposition of estate and gift tax. Often called a charitable remainder trust (CRT).

Charitable Lead Trust

This type of trust is often used for estate purposes and tax efficiency.

Charitable Remainder Trust (CRT)

This is an irrevocable trust whereas the funds are transferred to the designated charity after death or the settlor or at a chosen time. There is also a more complex CRT trust called a Charitable Remainder Trust Retirement Fund.

Special Needs Trust

Often used as a way around losing eligibility for SSI or Medicaid is to create what's called special needs or supplemental needs trust. This is very common for disabled children who will survive into adulthood and for medical and health related care.

Domestic Asset Protection Trust

The DAPT is created in states that have anti-creditor trust acts (Alaska, Delaware, South Dakota, Nevada, and some others) and allows an individual to establish a trust for his or her own assets that offers protection from creditors.

Asset Protection Trust

A trust is protected by creditors, so long as the trust is not created fraudulently, or to fraudulently convey any assets.

United Kingdom Trusts[3]

In the United Kingdom you have the Channel Islands which serve as an offshore financial center, and a major fiduciary.

---

[3]Common trusts types listed at Companies House.

Bare Trusts

Assets in a bare trust are held in the name of a trustee. However, the beneficiary has the right to all of the capital and income of the trust at any time if they're 18 or over (in England and Wales), or 16 or over (in Scotland). This means the assets set aside by the settlor will always go directly to the intended beneficiary.

Interest-in-Possession Trusts

These are trusts where the trustee must pass on all trust income to the beneficiary as it arises (less any expenses).

Discretionary Trusts

These are where the trustees can make certain decisions about how to use the trust income, and sometimes the capital.

Accumulation Trusts

This is where the trustees can accumulate income within the trust and add it to the trust's capital. They may also be able to pay income out, as with discretionary trusts.

Settlor-Interested Trusts

The settlor or their spouse or civil partner benefits from the trust. The trust is usually one of these three types of trusts: interest in possession trust; accumulation trust or discretionary trusts.

Non-Resident Trusts

This is a trust where the trustees are not residents of the United Kingdom for tax purposes.

Life Interest Trust

A beneficiary is given an interest in trust assets for their lifetime, usually the entitlement to receive income, and/or live in a property owned by the trust.

Waqf

A waqf is a trustee instrument created in the medieval period. It is very similar to a trust but its use is quite limited to the Islamic world. Waqfs are intended to last forever; depending on the regional laws the agreement may be terminated, dissolved or and principle or property given to the waqf returned to the creator or the creators' heirs.

Foundations

> What is the difference between a private foundation and a public charity? Every Sect. 501(c)(3) organization is classified as either a private foundation or a public charity. Private foundations and public charities are distinguished primarily by the level of public involvement in their activities. Public charities generally receive a greater portion of their financial support from the general public or governmental units, and have greater interaction with the public. A private foundation, on the other hand, is typically controlled by members of a family or by a small group of individuals, and derives much of its support from a small number of sources and from investment income. Because they are less open to public scrutiny, private foundations are subject to various operating restrictions and to excise taxes for failure to comply with those restrictions. Under the tax law, a Sect. 501(c)(3) organization is presumed to be a private foundation unless it requests, and qualifies for, a ruling or determination as a public charity.—Internal Revenue Service[4]

Often there is a tremendous interest in preserving legacies. As many know, a foundation, a charitable foundation, or a charitable trust is the most common tool for a family to plan worldwide. While they differ across the world according to civil law or common law, the concept remains the same with the exceptions of a charitable trust in England almost always being set up for charitable purposes, much like an endowment in the American world.

[4]IRS, EO Operational Requirements: Private Foundations and Public Charities.

Wealthy families often use foundations to hold assets and own assets. It is not unusually for a wealthy family to have multiple foundations. Family foundations and funds can operate as fully endowed entities with a full staff and leadership hierarchy, as well as operating on a fund basis driven by volunteers or that of a small private foundation run by a few people on a part-time basis. It all depends on the purpose of the foundation. Establishing and managing private foundations are not ways to cheat your taxes or to classify as a charity or non-profit (though many go on to establish charitable funds, endowments, and foundations active in fundraising); foundations are built on the core value of preservation and providing for certain entities and beneficiaries.

Additionally there are options and different ways to fund foundations: from fine arts, jewelry, and trusts holding royalties (broadcast; copyrights; oil rights; syndicated loans and securities).

While private foundations are often are the backbones of family offices, large privately funded foundations have built some of American greatest cities and regions. When a foundation is instrumental in supporting vast change and development like the Cullen Foundation of Houston, the Woodruff Foundation of Atlanta; the Ford Foundation of New York City; the Nemours Foundation of Jacksonville; or the Duke Endowment of North Carolina, these institutions have kept on and remained significant, often growing tremendously and even dominating discussions on their future plans and new leaders much like corporate giants. For instance, the Duke Endowment was founded on December 11, 1924, when James Buchanan Duke established a perpetual trust. In it he paced $40 million dollars, the 2020 equivalent to $594,159,537.57. James B. Duke set up his endowment in perpetuity; the Duke Endowment is guided by and adheres to the indenture of trust set forth by James B. Duke. It has been modified a few times by the Supreme Court of Mecklenburg County, North Carolina. The Alfred I. duPont trust is of equal state and national importance.

Alfred I. DuPont

The Alfred I. duPont Testamentary Trust funds one beneficiary (to my knowledge) which is the Nemours Foundation. The foundation and network is located in Jacksonville, Florida, and upon Alfred's death, he bequeathed the equivalent of $1.72 billion (in 2014 dollars). The fund has continued to be successful and has distributed more than $3 billion in support to the Nemours Foundation over the last 80 years. Today the foundation holds between $4 and 5B in assets. While charity support of the Nemours Foundation has been the number one goal of this trust, the caretakers seemingly have been excellent stewards of wealth and long-term fiduciary planning.

> It has been my firm conviction throughout life that it is the duty of everyone in the world to do what is within his power to alleviate human suffering. It is, therefore, natural that I should desire after having made provision for the immediate members of my family and others whom I have seen fit to remember, that the remaining portion of my estate be utilized for charitable needs.—Statement from the Alfred I. duPont Testamentary Trust

The Nemours Foundation is the charity that receives the yearly investment income from the Alfred I. duPont Charitable Trust. Nemours is one of the largest pediatric healthcare systems in the United States. Alfred Mr. duPont's will mandated that a charity was established to develop the treatment for children and also for the benefit of the elderly. By 1940, the foundation opened its first children's health program and by the 1960s, the foundation had become widely respected in pediatrics. By the 1990s, Nemours Children's Clinics were located in Delaware, Pensacola and Orlando, Florida.

Zaha Hadid Foundation

Zaha was a famous British-Iraqi architect and designer who died without immediate heirs (she never married or had children). When she died, she left her shares of her professional practice (Zaha Hadid Architects) in trust. To accompany the trust or trusts, Zaha also had a foundation, the Zaha Hadid Foundation. Hadid gave her executors and the foundation trustees—who are the same people—a lot of power, including the ability to add beneficiaries and a long distribution schedule—up to 125 years from the time of her death to disburse the estate, valued at around $80M.

If executors do not agree on how the estate should be distributed, or take no action within 125 years, it will pass to the Zaha Hadid Foundation. However, executors may face a legal challenge if they do not distribute the estate in the best interests of beneficiaries.

The Fuggerei

> In every decision we make for the Fuggerei, we try to consider that and be prudent. It would be disastrous if a mistake brought sustainability to an end after 19 generations.—Count Alexander Fugger-Babenhausen

I know Alex Fugger, the current Count Fugger-Babenhausen. His family story is remarkable for many reasons. He is a descendant of Jacob Fugger, who eventually became the richest man of the sixteenth century. He made his fortune in a variety of ways and became one of the most important forces in continental Europe. With his vast wealth, he established the Fuggerei in 1521 which was to be the first public subsidized house in the world. In exchange for a rent, tenants are to say prayers three times a day for the soul of the founder and his family. The prayers are the Lord's Prayer, Hail Marys, and the Nicene Creed. A tour of the property costs more than the annual rent. The great-grandfather of Wolfgang Amadeus Mozart, Franz Mozart lived in the Fuggerei between 1681 and 1694.

The Fuggerei is supported by a charitable trust established in 1520 which Jakob Fugger funded with an initial deposit of the historical equivalent of 10,000 guilders. According to the Wall Street Journal, the trust has been carefully managed with most of its income coming from forestry holdings, which the Fugger family has favored since the seventeenth century after losing money on higher yielding investments. The annual return on the trust has ranged from an after-inflation rate of 0.5 to 2%. The Fugger family foundation is administered by three branches of the Fugger family, Thun-Fugger, Fugger-Babenhausen and Fugger von Glött.

Harvard University

Harvard Corporation, the corporate body supporting and governing Harvard College (1636) is arguably the oldest corporation in the Western Hemisphere. I mention Harvard because the college was named after John Harvard, one of America's oldest philanthropists. John was born in 1607 in Southwark, London and immigrated to America where he settled in Charlestown, Massachusetts, just east of Cambridge where Harvard University lies. John Harvard ended up dying very young, at age 30 of tuberculosis, but not before drawing up a will bequeathing his library and half his financial resources to the little college in Cambridge on the Charles River. John Harvard's bequeath changed the world forever.

Bibliography

See the James Campbell Company LLC.
See Trust Companies, South Dakota Department of Labor & Regulation.
See Companies House UK for reference.
See Internal Revenue Service (IRS), EO Operational Requirements: Private Foundations and Public Charities.

9

Patronage and Collecting

Patronage

Patronage is a well-trodden path among the wealthy especially in the realms of fine art and culture. Without patrons we would not have many of the grand operas or symphonies we so enjoy. Art collections and collections at large are no different. When discussing fine art and purchasing investments, it is often said that art collecting is merely just collecting, all the while many make fortunes buying and selling artworks by blue-chip artists.

Such parallels exist in many of the connoisseur fields. Take wine for example, you will be hard-pressed to find a wine trader who doesn't appreciate fine wine enough to drink the choice selection themselves, versus sell it off or trade it. Such passions can create a sizable interest in the hands of smart people with means. A common thread is the ability to spend the money and invest the time in a second career of enjoyment, while organizing the framework as a business or investing enterprise so as to better track the allocations of funding, profits, and losses devoted to the endeavors. In this chapter, I will touch on the more common forms of patronages and collections.

Collections

It is well documented that wealthy families have collected valuable works of art, antiques, silver, automobiles, jewels, and heirlooms since antiquity. Rudimentary collections have been discovered in ancient society well before

C. Hagan, *Global Family Office Investing*,
https://doi.org/10.1007/978-3-030-18224-3_9

the days of antiquity, a prominent example would be the pyramids of Giza believed to be built for Khufu, the pharaoh monarch of Egypt. Collecting really began to develop during the days of the Hellenistic period and then with the Roman Empire; vases, decorative coins and medals (numismatics), reliefs and sculptures.

In Europe organized collecting of art, items of curiosity as well as funding the production of such works developed significantly during the Italian renaissance with further development from continental elites and English aristocrats embarking on their grand tour (a Western custom lasting from the mid-seventeenth century to the mid-nineteenth century).

As art patronage trickled down from the very, very wealthy to the bourgeois, purchasing famous and renowned pieces for personal possession was a way to flaunt wealth. It was also a great strategy to capture cultural capital. During the demise of France's Ancien Régime, priceless artworks were passed from French households to British households and further to American households, resulting in one of the most significant transfers of cultural capital in modern times.

I have spoken about differences in values and appreciation inside family offices, family business, family foundations and holdings but not of the more erudite examples of wealth and culture. Howard Lewis of the Schorr Collection puts an emphasis on passion and the living spirit of the family, in accordance with a loose framework of goals and management. He is after all the leading second generation so there is a bit of expertise and legacy drive within his own vision and daily life. Additionally, it is equally important to realize the family-owned collection and the heirs that may become inherited curators.

Howard is not at all worried about the up-and-coming generations within his family and their love of art. They either love it or they don't. If they do there they have an excellent platform, but he is a realist and prepared for the collection to continue with or without the next generations' support. To date, the Schoor Collection has half of the collection's pieces on long-term loans at home and abroad. This aspect is one of the more important ethos of family offices I have discovered the will to continue with or without an obsession over future governance. It is as if the most successful family offices are the ones who accept the fate of the family office and family legacy.

> The creation of a private collection is an intensely personal exercise. The objects so gathered would exist whether or not brought together in one ownership. Such a collection may reflect the vanity of the collector, or it may, hopefully, reflect an intellectual curiosity which can to some extent be satiated by the juxtaposition of period, style, subject, medium, artist or creator.

This fulfils a subjective desire to learn and appreciate in the comfort and accessibility of one's own possessions, rather than within the public domain. However, the private rather than public satisfaction of intellectual curiosity contains an inevitable element of vanity. Artistic endeavour whether from a composer, writer, poet, architect, sculptor, artist, belongs in the public domain. Ownership is ephemeral, but the act of private ownership is itself an endeavour which can provide an insight into the very process of selection and acquisition.—David Lewis, Foreword from The Schorr Collection (Vol 1 and 2).

Investing in New Frontiers

Family offices are by nature long-term investors and focused around returns, fiduciary sensibilities and planning, and customized esoteric methods. The wealthy often push pet projects and personal interests, running in parallel to ancient benefactors of arts and exploration: Columbus has his royal sponsors; The 5th Earl of Carnarvon financed the expedition that discovered King Tut. The sinister and occult-laden Allister Crowley financed his own mountain climbing expeditions off his family's brewing fortune. He ventured as far as K2, and it was wildly disastrous, but he became famous for it. Additionally, how many of the upper classes have flocked to new technology and new mediums since the creation of the photograph? When the upper class begins to swarm around trends, products, and schools of thought, it is often a harbinger of things to come; so, it is no surprise the wealthy bankroll expeditions. The connection between money, curiosity, and exploration is nothing new but in the modern age, we are beginning to see an entirely new form of adventure and expeditionary travel. The world of oceans and space is now dominated by billionaires and titans but if this is any hint at what the future may bring you can count on an engaged public and an even more engaged and educated group of citizen scientists. The country of Monaco employed Jacques-Yves Cousteau from 1957–1988 and was bolstered by the support of Prince Albert I who devoted much of his life to the study of the ocean and led many expeditions from his customized expedition yachts.

Exploration as Profession

A fortune of any size can help accomplish many things but more than often fortunes, family businesses and family offices help accommodate for the extra things we want in life. When I was first married, my wife and I took a lot of mountaineering expeditions. My parents had allowed me to go on a few backpacking expeditions in my teenage years but I was never able to vanish into the mountain in the way that I wanted to. There were a lot of other things involved in the expeditions and I enjoyed handling the logistics of the trip and there was an immense payoff, which combined authentic experiences, far-flung travel, photography, and plenty of writing material on travel, nature, food, and exploration. I became involved in the Explores Club (NYC) and the American Alpine Club and was able to interact with legends of the sport. Eventually I stopped climbing because we had to plan longer expeditions to acclimate to the higher altitudes, among other things, but I am grateful my wife and I took those trips in our late 20s and early 30s. Above all, I was able to cross a few crazy expeditions off the list; I was able to devote a lot of time to a passion. Let's switch roles for a moment and pretend that I am a 60-year man who has worked every day since college and now I have the fortune to spend and I am looking to make up for the lost time. If you take Hollywood mega director James Cameron, it doesn't take long to see how the synergies of his success could easily equate to groundbreaking discovery and success in exploration. Cameron has pushed the boundaries in exploration and technology, thereby creating new crafts and new microtechnologies. While it could be said that he is pursuing his life passion, he is very influential and his focus on deep-sea exploration or shipwreck recovery is much bigger than just one man's dream. In fact, Cameron has surpassed filmmaking and has become a bona fide explorer. He has even been part of the Woods Hole Institute, which is one of the world's most celebrated ocean institutes.

A similar situation can be found with Falkor. The former Google executive Eric Schmidt has an ocean research institute and he houses the institute on the institute's vessel, which is named Falkor. The vessel is a research vessel and is close to 300 feet long. The venture is a 501(c)(3) foundation dedicated to advanced oceanographic research and sharing data on ocean health. In this case, the free market has stepped up and taken a tremendous burden off of grant funding and fundraising for science.

Second Voyage of HMS Beagle

The voyage of Charles Darwin on the HMS Beagle is one of the most famous scientific expeditions in human history, but it did not come together haphazardly. While aspects of the voyage came down to fate, a young and highly connected British officer in the Royal navy, Robert FitzRoy, had been given lead control of a second expedition to survey South America due to ambition and family connections, FitzRoy was also a scientist and he wanted scientists on the voyage and asked "that some well-educated and scientific person should be sought who would willingly share such accommodations as I could offer, in order to profit by the opportunity of visiting distant countries yet little known."[1] Enter the young Charles Darwin, who after some lobbying joined the expedition; Darwin's father had to partial pay Charles' way, only room and board was provided by the Royal Navy. Both Darwin and FitzRoy were from established and well-bred backgrounds. FitzRoy was a great-grandson of Charles II and a grandson of the 3rd Duke of Grafton, he also had a stable of powerful uncles in politics and society looking after his success and his father was a wealthy society doctor and financier. Darwin was a grandson of Josiah Wedgewood, the famed pottery entrepreneur and founder of Wedgewood and Sons, and paternal grandfather of Erasmus Darwin.

NASA Strategic Technology Investment Plan

Spurred on by NASA joint ventures and investment opportunities, NASA has released investments it sees as a critical technology needed for space travel and development.

Below is a Critical Technology Investments listing, from NASA's STIP program:

> Critical Technology Investments: NASA has identified ten broad investment areas containing Critical technologies. These areas group the Critical technologies from one or more of the 2015 NASA Technology Roadmap areas. Critical technologies identified in the 2015 NASA Technology Roadmaps are generally cross-cutting, meet more than one mission-specific need, and provide significant risk reduction. Critical technologies also include aeronautics research thrusts. NASA's investment in Critical technologies will comprise approximately 70 percent of the Agency's technology development portfolio. These technologies have a crucial enabling role for NASA's scientific, robotic, and human exploration missions. The ten Critical technology investment areas are:
>
> 1. Propulsion and Launch Systems
> 2. Human Health, Life Support, and Habitation
> 3. Destination Systems
> 4. Robotics and Autonomous Systems

[1] Rice, Tony. "Voyage of Discovery." Natural History Museum. London, England. 2000. Page 230.

5. Scientific Instruments, Sensors, and Optical Communications
6. Lightweight Space Structures and Materials
7. Entry, Descent, and Landing
8. Space Power Systems
9. Advanced Information Systems
10. Aeronautics[2]

I spoke with a friend of mine, the global explorer and social entrepreneur Guillermo Sohnlein. He was kind enough to contribute an overview of recent family offices oriented expeditions, as well as include an expedition checklist.

> Given the variety of funding channels for explorers and expeditions, every family office can craft an exploration component specifically suited to its portfolio. A few examples offer a representative view of what is possible in modern exploration, for example, Elon Musk's SpaceX; Jeff Bezos' Blue Origin; Richard Branson's Virgin Galactic; Robert Bigelow's Bigelow Aerospace; Ray Dalio's OceanX; Eric Schmidt's Schmidt Ocean Institute; Victor Vescovo's Five Deeps Expedition.
>
> Sea—Belize Blue Hole[3]
>
> In December 2018, a group of 70+ explorers, scientists, filmmakers, conservationists, submersible pilots, engineers, and equipment operators conducted a two-week expedition to one of the world's largest underwater caverns, the Belize Blue Hole. Organized and led by Aquatica Submarines (a Vancouver-based company that builds, sells, and operates manned submersibles), the mission achieved a number of significant objectives, including creating a 3D sonar map of the entire cavern. Most significant, the funding for the expedition came from a diversified pool of sources, including corporate sponsors, production companies, nonprofit organizations, government agencies, and individual "tourists."
>
> Earth—Masaya Volcano[4]
>
> In August 2016, explorer Sam Cossman[5] and former NASA astronaut Scott Parazynski[6] became the first humans to descend into the mouth of one of Nicaragua's most active volcanoes. The primary purpose was to deploy a network of sensors that scientists could use as early detection to protect local communities from future eruptions. Although the Nicaraguan government

[2]NASA STIP 2017.

[3]Aquatica Submarines Inc. (Belize Blue Hole Expedition).

[4]GE "A Digital Volcano".

[5]Sam Cossman, Explorer.

[6]Scott E Parazynski.

provided some operational and logistical support, the expedition was funded by General Electric, which also provided the technology for the sensor network.

Space—The Moon[7]

In February 2019, an Israeli nonprofit organization named SpaceIL launched the world's first privately funded lunar mission. When it arrives at its destination in April 2019, the small robot is scheduled to perform two days of data collection. If successful, it will make Israel only the fourth country (behind Russia, the United States, and China) to successfully land a mission on the surface of the Moon. Despite a long list of corporate partners and supporters, the mission was primarily funded by individual major donors.

Project Outline:

Step 1—Understand the Family's Objectives

The best way for a family office to venture into exploration is to make sure those efforts connect with the overall family office strategy and structure. The most important question is, "why does the family office want to include exploration in its portfolio?" This leads to a number of other relevant questions:

- Are there financial drivers, or is it more of a personal passion?
- Are there specific geographic or scientific areas of interest?
- How much do the family members want to be actively involved in exploration efforts?
- How will exploration connect with the other elements of the family office?
- How much of a focus will exploration be within the overall family office portfolio?
- What resources can the family office offer to the exploration community?

Step 2—Develop a Strategy

Once the preliminary context is set, a proper exploration strategy can be developed. depending on the family office requirements, there are three primary paths:

- *Investment.* If well-organized, exploration expeditions can be profitable ventures, even if nominally. Most expeditions have some media creation component, which can also be funded separately as an investment vehicle. Others may present opportunities to commercialize innovative "dual-use" technologies originally invented to support exploration. Finally, one or more of a family office's portfolio companies may be strategic brand sponsors for certain missions.

[7] SpaceIL.

- *Donation.* There are many exploration-focused nonprofit organizations that could benefit from private donations or a *family foundation's grants. These might be exploration-specific or more likely generally science-, education-, and conservation-based. Also, there are many individual explorers developing concepts for new expeditions and scientists crafting new field research ideas, and all of them could benefit from a family office benefactor.*
- *Participation.* This is perhaps the most exciting recent development, since there is a growing number of opportunities for funders to actively participate in exploration expeditions without having to actually be explorers or expedition leaders (or to fully finance the entire expedition). As "Citizen Scientists" or "Citizen Explorers", family members can financially support exploration while also becoming an integral part of the expedition team, in some cases even receiving technical or scientific training as part of the role.

Step 3—Implement

The implementation plan will obviously depend on the specific strategy, especially how much of a public commitment the family wants to make toward exploration. On one end of the spectrum, a few family offices create their own exploration companies, nonprofits, or programs. On the other end of the spectrum, many family offices make quiet financial contributions to existing initiatives. There is a wide range in between, with some becoming major public supporters of certain organizations or missions and with some actively participating in their individual capacities. Regardless, the best way to implement a strategy is to break inertia and start delving into the exploration community. By its very nature, exploration is a fluid human activity, so the most important way to get a family office involved is to dip toes in the water and see where it leads.

Step 4—Refine

Exploration changes people in very fundamental ways. Once a family office adds exploration to its portfolio, it needs to continually review, evaluate, and modify its activities. It is critical to collect data, map them against success metrics, and adopt updates as needed. Sometimes initial forays into exploration scare family offices away from future activities, but often it fuels a strong desire to add more. A strong feedback loop is crucial to maintaining balance and discipline within the portfolio.

Aeronautics and Aviation

Wealthy individuals and by nature their families can be found in the world of aviation. Much like the world of automobiles, families are collectors, pilots and of course passengers in the world of planes, jets, and experimental aircraft. In the past, a sure way for a love of aeronautics was the services, but that is no longer common in most developed countries, especially America. In the higher population areas of North America (NYC, Los Angeles, Chicago, Mexico City, and Toronto) private aircraft are plentiful—like supercars & super yachts—and there is quite a bit of availability of private aircraft like helicopters, small planes, and jets. This is because of the markets associated with the population which guarantee traffic and people willing to spend large sums to get out immediately. The presence of large corporations almost guarantees the use of private jets, as private corporations can easily shoulder erroneous travel expenses.

On expenses: wealthy people have the budget to fuel passions, and while the cost of flying has been dropping over each decade, it is still expensive to keep anything other than an ultra-light small aircraft. This expenditure has led to cottage industries of aircraft leasing, both wet and dry leasing and aircraft specialty finance to help ease the burden of an aircraft. The difference between leasing or purchasing aircraft often comes down to the financial needs of the buyer. Lease payments are classified as business expenses; financing a jet for a purchase can be used as a large tax write-off in the United States, but you will need specialist skills[8] to resell the aircraft. In North America, leasing allows the owner to arrange certain terms, which may allow multiple aircraft[9] and wet or dry leasing:

Wet Aircraft Lease:
It is turnkey; you rent the services of the plane—meaning: the fuel, crew, associated costs are essentially provided for and one does not need associated regulatory licensing.

Dry Aircraft Lease:
This is not a turnkey lease and it for the more experienced; you lease the aircraft, but you bring everything else, including associated regulatory licensing.

Yachting and Sailing

The wealthy have been boating for eons. Today it largely depends on the culture of the region, but the tradition is alive and well and very popular in the family office world. Small lakes, large lakes, coastline, ports, broad rivers,

[8]Much like the world of yachting, the aircraft world has little shortage of qualified specialists.
[9]This is not in reference to private jet cards or prepaid hours.

and wetlands all command different types of maritime culture and therefore different types of boats. Regardless, boating and associated activities are very popular and the family office world is no exception. The ultra-wealthy routinely build mega-yachts and seasonal charters are highly sought-after commodities in certain urban areas. As mentioned earlier with Price Albert, yachting, whether for science or leisure, can be a lifelong activity, and there is potential for profit making, if only to break-even on the associated costs.

Sailing is perhaps a more approachable aspect to yachting due to its sporting nature and regattas complete with luxury brand sponsorships and full-blown parties. As a sport, the regattas and competitions are very social and participants tend to live maritime-oriented lifestyles and be employed, or have business and investments in associated industries.

Automobiles

This goes without saying; there is no shortage of wealthy car collectors, to the extent that the market is so liquid you can all but guarantee trades with some makes and models. The sheer amount of luxury and collector automobile auctions per season is staggering, with record amounts turning over year after year. The automobile industry is taking note. At this point, the American automobile market has pivoted to that of manufacturing bigger SUVs with eye watering sticker prices; at the same time limiting production on sedans and commuter cars. Electric vehicles may dominate the discussion but at this very moment, the major automobile manufacturers are making bigger and more expensive vehicles each year. The major manufacturers often move in similar style with one another. The reason I mention this is because it helps support my observation; the automobile industry is maturing, it is expanding, it is indispensable. The automotive industry is developing to the point that the expense of the product, whatever it may be, will most certainly be borrowed, financed, or leased, and with the sticker price rationalized in the consumers' mind the possibilities are endless. At this moment we are moving toward electrically powered driverless cars. The fact is that the industry is maturing to the point that is becoming unrecognizable from its origins. Cars are mementos of transportation history. Antique cars are relics of society. If you know what you are doing, in the used car market and antique market, returns will be realized. Expect antique car prices to continue to rise, expect new models to get bigger, and expect electric vehicles to push sticker prices to new levels.

Conservation, Landowning, and Environmentalism

North of Inverness, Scotland 150 miles is Alladale, the 23,000 acres estate where Paul Lister spends his summers and plots his latest endeavors. The estate contains seven lakes (or lochs), a number of stream and river ways, and an ever growing cache of wildlife and wild foliage.

Paul purchases Alladale in 2003 and immediately set to turning the vast swath of wilderness back to its original form. His estate boats Golden Eagle, White Tailed Eagle, Red Squirrel, Wild Boar, Elk, Red Deer, and the addition of over 900,000 trees. His devotion to reestablishing a natural ecosystem with apex predators has neighbors calling him the wolf man.

Long ago in Scotland, there exists the Caledonian forest. For thousands of years—if not more—Caledonian pine forests covered loch sides and glens. Today only a small fragment remains. "Caledonian, or native pinewoods, are characterized by an open woodland canopy and dispersed trees. Species include Scots pine, juniper, birch, willow, rowan and aspen. They grow on infertile soils and are a link to the huge boreal forests of Scandinavia and Northern Russia. They support rare, specialist species."[10]

Eurasian wolves were hunted out by the mid-eighteenth century; beavers were driven out by the nineteenth century; the last of Britain's wild bears have been gone for over 2,000 years ago.

At Allandale, there is plenty of room for the Eurasian elk, which is a Moose in North American, and wild lynx—which was said to have left the United Kingdom by 250 AD.

Paul is the founder of The European Nature Trust (TENT) which is a registered charity focused on wildlife films, and communications surrounding wildlife projects in Europe—Paul's environmental philanthropy extends to cover Spain, Romania, and Italy. He is a world traveler who has a strong entrepreneurial attitude, as Allandale has expanded to offer yoga, mindfulness retreats, venison, and ecological cosmetics, in addition to luxury nature hospitality.

One of the first British landowners to devote their estate to rewilding and ecological sovereignty was Charlie Burrell, also known as Sir Charles Burrell, 10th Baronet. Sir Charles lives with his family at Knepp Castle in West Sussex. It is from here he has launched his assault on industrial farming after nearly running the ancestral farmlands into bankruptcy after an expensive failed attempt of establishing a sustainable working farm. Charl4is as

[10]The Woodland Trust (United Kingdom).

his family concluded that it was simply not possible to run a profitable and sustainable working farm at Knepp. A report by English Nature, which is the UK Government agency behind the conservation of wildlife and geology throughout England, established an in-deopth narrative regarding farming at Knepp in, "following World War II, the Knepp Castle Estate was, in common with much of southern England, under increasingly intensive arable management. The decision of its owner, Charlie Burrell, to return the Estate to a more natural environment has resulted in some 322 hectares being taken out of arable cultivation and instead grazed with a low number of cattle, pigs, ponies and deer. Intervention is minimal within compliance with UK legislation. The interest in conservation grazing and near-natural grazing and the differences between these two systems is currently high, following Frans Vera's book Grazing Ecology and Forest History and the debate that this publication has subsequently engendered. However there are many as yet unanswered questions regarding how a near-natural system might operate in 21st Century Europe, despite the seminal example of Oostvaardersplassen in the Netherlands. By moving a considerable way towards near-natural grazing, the Knepp Castle Estate presents the chance to explore some of these issues."[11]

To free himself of the loss, Charlie turns the land over to nature. In December 2002, Burrell launched his vision for rewilding Knepp and sent a Letter of Intent to Natural England—which is the government's advisory body for the environment, setting out his plans to establish "A Biodiverse Wilderness Area in the Low Weald of Sussex." He brought in free-roaming herds of old English longhorns, Exmoor ponies, Tamworth pigs, red deer, and fallow deer and he established an advisory board of leading naturalists, ecologists, and environmentalists to see it thorough. The project took years and years of devotion, but in 2012, the Knepp Wildland project received Higher Level Stewardship funding in the United Kingdom.

Charlie still farms, but it is far more direct and also organic and he has added other resources like Paul Lister to add to the allure of his estate. Glamping and cam[poing as well as nature safaris. The Knepp Wildland species include nightingales; white storks, turtle doves, purple emperor butterflies, all the UK species of owls, and nearly all of the United Kingdom's 17 species of bats.

[11]English Nature Research Reports, Number 693, "Knepp Castle Estate baseline ecological survey".

Case Study: The Wallace Collection

Sometimes collecting is one's main career and profession. The Wallace Collection was formed by four generations of the Hertford and Wallace family; Largely pioneered by the 4th Marquess of Hertford and Sir Richard Wallace (the illegitimate son of the fourth Marquess), between the 1780s and the 1880s.

The 4th Marquess and his out-of-wedlock son, Sir Richard Wallace, conspired to create one of the great public art collections of the modern age. They did so with complete disregard to the social order at the time. Lord Hertford died in 1870, and the baronetcy passed to his distant cousin. His only son, Richard Wallace received the unentitled estate which included the art collection, and numerous other fortunes. It is often reported that Richard was unaware he was Lord Hertford's son, despite working for him as a secretary while building one of the grandest art collections the world has ever seen and despite being raised by Lord Hertford's mother. To complicate matters, Richard had been forbidden to marry the mother of his only child while Lord Hertford was alive.

It was said the 4th marquess once declared, "when I die I shall at least have the consolation of knowing that I have never rendered anyone a service."[12] Nevertheless, Lord Hertford did a fabulous service by leaving his collection to the nation and ultimately the world.

Sir Richard was different from his father. He was said to be charismatic and warmhearted, generous to the point of being famous in France. In 1870, during the Franco-Prussian War, Wallace was in Paris and had just inherited his father's unentitled estate, Wallace design and financed water foundations for the poor. He wanted them to be beautiful and useful, not only works of art but water foundation that could supply the poor with clean water, to detour the lower classes from drinking only liquor, beer and wine. This simple gesture has created a global ripple effect with Wallace Fountains collected by collectors and institutions worldwide.

Since 1870, the collection has been housed in Hertford House, long a mainstay of the Hertford family, and one of the residences Wallace and his father used for storage. The Wallace family collection was largely made up of French pieces bought during the regime change during the French Revolution. His father, the marquis, and his Hertford ancestors were uniquely positions to acquire priceless pieces of work disemboweled from France's

[12]Edmond de Goncourt, Jules de Goncourt, Pages from the Goncourt Journal, translated by Robert Baldick, New York Review of Books, 2007, page 154 (14 August 1869).

grand collections. While Wallace had the deepest ties to France and Paris, his collection was left to the people and nation of England.

The Collection was bequeathed to the British Nation by Lady Wallace in 1897, "lady Wallace's bequest states that the collection 'shall be kept together unmixed with other objects of art'. This has traditionally been understood to mean that the Collection can neither acquire, nor can it deaccession, any work of art. By extension, this has also been understood to mean that the Wallace Collection cannot exhibit works from elsewhere alongside its own. The museum contains Old Master paintings, miniatures, sculpture, French furniture, porcelain and goldsmiths' work, European, African and Asian arms and armour, and medieval and Renaissance works of art. All are of the highest quality and of international importance. Its holdings of French eighteenth-century art, European princely arms and armory and Old Master paintings are recognized internationally as being outstanding."[13]

Bibliography

Rice, Tony. "Voyage of Discovery." Natural History Museum. London, England. 2000.

See English Nature Research Reports, Number 693, "Knepp Castle Estate baseline ecological survey".

See Edmond de Goncourt, Jules de Goncourt, Pages from the Goncourt Journal, translated by Robert Baldick, New York Review of Books, 2007, page 154 (14 August 1869).

[13]The Wallace Collection, Hertford House, London, W1U 3BN.

Bibliography.

(1) Rice, Tony. "Voyage of Discovery." Natural History Museum. London, England. 2000.

10–11) See English Nature Research Reports, Number 693, "Knepp Castle Estate baseline ecological survey".

(12) See Edmond de Goncourt, Jules de Goncourt, Pages from the Goncourt Journal, translated by Robert Baldick, New York Review of Books, 2007, page 154 (14 August 1869).

10

The Future of Family Offices

New Wealth on the Horizon

After a decade of research and field work, I have been able to patch together an independent snapshot of global family offices. As one can imagine, clustering of family offices occurs in financial capitals, so in theory, family offices are present from a global perspective in every substantial regional economic hub. This also means there is a lack of family offices where there is a lack of economic sophistication. The rich world is inherently interconnected, and we can expect to see a surge in Asian, Indian, and Russian family offices in the future, these are the latest wealth and gathering of fortunes that need protection and management. It is in the aforementioned parts of the world that I foresee some of the greatest change ahead in family wealth and ultimately global influence.

Straightened by Sanctions and Friction

I cannot think of a different mix of peoples and nations than what encompasses the Middle East, Russia, and Central Asia. In the Middle East, apart from North Africa, the development is scattered throughout many tribes and countries often at war or in collaboration with. For that reason alone the Middle East, Russia, & Central Asia are grouped together for good reason. A tremendous amount of the countries in these regions are under sanction or embattled in war and overlapping concerns and worries.

C. Hagan, *Global Family Office Investing*,
https://doi.org/10.1007/978-3-030-18224-3_10

You can think of the Middle East as a bit of an experiment with territorial issues. The experiment was first created by the Europeans and then taken over and managed by the Americans. Both parties wanted the regional oil supplies and both parties were able to secure the oil commodities by subsequently inheriting a lot of the problems from the area. In hindsight, the EU stayed the protectorate of Iran and the United States stayed the protectorate of Saudi Arabia and the Saud royal family. That has created a vacuum of geopolitical partisanship to such a degree that it is hard to clearly hear both sides of the story. Regardless, the two mega powers in the Middle East are Saudi Arabia and Iran and they largely control much of the area. Kuwait, UAE, Qatar, and Bahrain—while vastly wealthy—lack the size to push much weight around in their domestic theater.

Structures

A tremendous amount of associated planning and family office structures for Central Asian and Middle East families are located in London, Geneva, or Singapore. As I will mention in this chapter, some are much further ahead than others. Geneva, Switzerland is coordinated in a particular diplomatic fashion where professionals can bridge the fractured and often sanctioned countries of Russia, Iran, and the rest of the world so that a continuation in business can be found. The Middle East, Russia, and Central Asia contain a deep cultural fabric of nations huddled together and conflicted authoritative regimes harboring immense natural resources wealth. Some MENA countries pay citizen dividends, particularly those with large gas reserves, and this creates a vast amount of loyalty.

Israel and Lebanon are quite developed for the region. Both have correspondence services with globally recognized banks and banks with branches in New York City or London. Israel has a booming technology and venture capital sector, as well as a developing hedge fund sector. In Israel, many banks have branches here, from JPM to Bank of New York Mellon. Beirut, Lebanon has been called the Paris of the Middle East but it is largely ruled by Arabian banks. Bank Audi is the largest bank in Lebanon and has a prominent New York City branch. Some banks have correspondence relations with major English-speaking banks but many are MENA oriented and associated with Qatar, Bahrain, or Saudi Arabia. Bahrain is considered an offshore zone to a degree and there are numerous family offices operating here from petroleum wealth but the region serves mostly Arab families.

If we take Saudi Arabia for example, outside the royal family business and enterprise is still managed in a concession form like a formalized cartel to a degree. Executives make fortunes from running state enterprises or owning monopolistic concessions. In Saudi Arabia for instance, the concession to exclusively sell Toyota's is very big business, as the economy has not been previously hard wired to the global economic system. Because of this the owner of Saudi Arabia's Toyota concession is one of the richest men in the country.

It wasn't until March 3, 1938, that oil was discovered in Saudi Arabia. Before the Saudi Arabia discovery, a number of American concessions led by Standard Oil of California, oil groups from Texas and the east coast were exploring for oil in the Middle East. By this time, America was well behind and British concessions and syndicates were dominating the Middle East. Iran had established close relations with Britain and had formed the precursor to BP in 1908 after the discovery of oil at Masjed Soleyman County, Iran.

Many sectors in Iran are run by the state or with the state's help. As one can imagine the families of the political class are often rewarded with riches, either legitimate or illegitimate. Iran's 2017 GDP, according to World Bank estimates, was $447B. It is no surprise that the U.S. has little to do with Iran, instead, Iran's heavily mixed economy, in which the state intervenes to strengthen business at home, does plenty of business with Europe and the rest of the world.

Europe is still close to Iran, and as we see Iran develop, we will see Europe and their industrial families become more enriched. There is a lot of wealth in Iran, particularly Tehran, but in theory, it's all over as the country is run in a very different manner. Economist Suzanne Maloney has written extensively about the noble-born children of the elite often called the aghazadeh.

A number of European countries have joined forces to create a robust payment channel called INSTEX.

> France, Germany and the United Kingdom, in accordance with their resolute commitment and continued efforts to preserve the Joint Comprehensive Plan of Action (JCPOA) endorsed by United Nations Security Council resolution 2231, announce the creation of INSTEX SAS (Instrument for Supporting Trade Exchanges), a Special Purpose Vehicle aimed at facilitating legitimate trade between European economic operators and Iran. The E3 reaffirm that their efforts to preserve the economic provisions of the JCPOA are conditioned upon Iran's full implementation of its nuclear-related commitments, including full and timely cooperation with the IAEA. INSTEX will support legitimate European trade with Iran, focusing initially on the sectors most essential to the

> Iranian population – such as pharmaceuticals, medical devices and agri-food goods.[1]

Dubai and Abu Dubai, UAE are largely for Arabian-based families and residents of the states. In the past twenty-five years, Saudi Arabia has dominated the headlines and become a vast superpower. The wealth from the Saudi's is old by Middle East standards, and they have the finest of the finest handling their sovereign family offices, operating in financial capitals throughout the world (London, Paris, Geneva, Singapore). The newest billions and billionaires in the Middle East are likely those from the coffers of Qatar. Qatar has grown to own much of London's upmarket buildings (in the City of London) and even Harrods. A number of years ago a collection of supercars painted in Qatari national colors were booted outside Knightsbridge in what was an equally ostentatious and humorous display of wealth. Regardless, the Qatari wealth is grouped into a ruling family and that family is vastly powerful, vastly wealthy, and numerous in descendants. A shared similarity in Saudi Arabia, UAE, and Qatar is that if you are close to the princes you are generally enriched, this means iron glove or velvet glove; you must stay in their favor to remain in noble light.

A powerful display of such lopsided ways was displayed by MBS, Saudi's crown prince when he arraigned many of the extended princes to be detained, until ransoms or reparations back to the government—however you would like to look at it—were paid. The ripple effect felt worldwide by this was staggering—some of the wealthiest investors in the world were rounded up and detained in a luxury hotel, sleeping on mattresses on the ground using blankets to cover their faces from the press.

Moreover, the killing of Jamal Khashoggi on foreign soil in a Saudi Arabian embassy was equally ostentatious. Jamal was a columnist for the Washington Post and his family, was deeply connected to the establishment in Saudi Arabia. The fact that MBS has been implicated in the killing shows the true extent of the power the kingdom is willing to exercise. The Khashoggi family is well known worldwide, Jamal's aunt, Samira Khashoggi married Mohamed Al-Fayed, a former owner of Harrods. Their child Dodi died with Diana, Princess of Wales in 1997. Jamal's uncle was the famous arms dealer and bon vivant Adnan Khashoggi and his grandfather, Muhammad Khashoggi was the private doctor to King Abdul-Aziz Al Saud, the founder of modern Saudi Arabia, who is also the father of all current kings and their offspring (King Saud had 45 sons).

---

[1]Ministry for Europe and Foreign Affairs, Joint statement by the E3 Foreign Ministers Jean-Yves Le Drian (France), Heiko Maas (Germany), Jeremy Hunt (United Kingdom).

Altaic Language Zones: Turkey, Mongolia, Uzbekistan

From Southern Europe (Turkey) to the far edges of Siberia and China, a little-known mountain region has lent its name to a grouping of ancient and influential languages. The Altaic languages, named after the Altaic Mountains, which is a zone in Russia that touches Kazakhstan, China, Russia, and Mongolia, the region holds base to some 60 plus languages, all of which are interrelated. If you were to ever wonder if Turkey, Azerbaijani, and Crimea are connected, look no further than the shared language among the Turkish, the Azerbaijani, the Crimean Tatars, the Mongolians, Kazakh and Uzbek. While all of the regions share linguistics and geographic relations, they are fairly different with a heavy dose of Islamic devotion.

It is safe to say that a family office in these parts is a relatively new concept to outwardly celebrate. Ownership and inheritance is so tightly related families will own the business regardless, and of course regional and tribal inheritance laws come in the play. This seems to be the current mode of operation in Mongolia which for years seemed to be building toward that of a transparent model. In recent years, Mongolia has become more entrenched in a Russian and Chinese model however, plenty of families venture off to safer places to establish loosely connected. China's One Belt, One Road initiative will create numerous expansions in the otherwise isolated and developing countries. The aforementioned project is creating sizable waves of economic success and limitations on human rights. There is a clear possibility in wealth creation through the One Belt project, but it could mimic if not completely mirror mainland China's state capitalism model. It is important to note that many of the central Asian nations are buckling under pressure from Russia and China in various forms, economically, politically, and socially. The family offices that emerge from this area will take on Russian and Chinese cultural aspects, and largely place branch offices in one of those countries.

Developments in Russia

Take for instance, Russia. Russia, it can be said, is new to the family money game. Before modern privatization in Russia, entrepreneurs and businessmen were focused to smuggle goods into Russia and take advantage of arbitrage on common items like blue jeans.

It is no secret that Russia has used London as a safe haven and an espionage point. Despite the fact that Russians and their foreign problems are not as welcomed as they once were, Russian money is still awash in London. Russia has also developed greatly in the past decade, and while that may not always be accurately reflected in their domestic politics or economic measures, they are taking strides to empower their economy with a mix of strongman politics, state capitalism, and businesses run by government connected oligarchs.

The largest ethnic Russian populations outside of Russia exist in former Soviet states such as Kazakhstan, Belarus, Latvia, Uzbekistan, and Kyrgyzstan. The largest population—about six million can be found in Ukraine, which is also the most developed state of the aforementioned former Soviet states. Russia has been busy exporting its system to America and Britain but has been doing so in central Europe for some time now. Austria is a well-known haven in Central Europe for Russian money and business.

In many of these countries, war is a daily operation. As mentioned, a tremendous amount of associated planning and family office structure for Central Asian and Middle East families are located in London, Geneva, or Singapore. MENA families often venture to UAE or Lebanon for private banking and Bahrain for offshore. Israel has a very strong private banking and family office system. UAE is by far the most liberal. In the past, Cyprus and Russia had a particularly strong connection, but that has been tarnished as of late. Russia has a reputation problem that only Russia can solve and they did just that. In 2018, Russia announced they would begin offshore operations in special offshore zones. One is located in the former part of Prussia Kaliningrad Region and the other in the Far East at Russky Island, south of Vladivostok in the Sea of Japan. This is a move from China's playbook, albeit better maneuvered.

On June 08, 2018, the Ministry for the Development of the Russian Far East released the following information on Russian SAR's:

> Russian President Vladimir Putin signed a package of laws on the establishment of special administrative regions (SAR) on Russky Island in the Primorsky Krai and the island of Oktyabrsky in the Kaliningrad region. It is a package of seven federal laws aimed at creating two "offshore" zones in Russia. Vladimir Putin signed the federal law "On Special Administrative Regions in the Territories of the Kaliningrad Region and Primorsky Krai". This law provides for the peculiarities of the exercise of the powers of the state authorities in the territory of the special administrative region, the procedure for consideration of applications for activities as a participant of the special administrative region, the procedure for assigning the status of a member of the special administrative

> region and the conditions of the activities of participants of the special administrative region and the management company in the territory of the special administrative region.

It is important to note that Russian federal law specifies the procedure for accounting of rights to securities of foreign issuers.[2] It is not an entirely cut and dry process, and without experts who have long-standing ties into Russia and with Russian finances, issues will arise. However, this can all be viewed as a slow evolutionary process toward free markets and free thinking.

In August of the following year, Russia relaxed more laws for the Kaliningrad region:

> The Federal law of August 3, 2018 N 291-FZ "On special administrative regions in the territories of the Kaliningrad region and Primorsky Krai" Date of signature 3 August 2018 Posted on 6 Aug 2018 Shall enter into force on 3 August 2018. Adopted by the state Duma on July 26, 2018 Approved by the Federation Council on 28 July 2018.[3]

These may not seem like liberal policies but they are for Russia. With recent moves accepting the Russian Orthodox Church as the national religion for Russians by Putin, Russia is moving away from state communism. Does this mean we are going to see a turn to legitimate free markets? Not so fast. Their numbers are simply not there, the Russian economy is quite small relative to its population and land mass. In the book "Imperium by Ryszard Kapuściński" the author takes the reader on a journey across Russia, through the cities and through the tundra. I was struck by the sheer space Russia encompasses, the time zones and the various cultures. As an American, the vastness of Russia appeals to me, it is like the vastness of America, the difference in their tundra and Siberia is our merely Wild West and Alaska. With all the sprawling space Russia has, if Putin is to create a stronger national identity, if he turns to the free markets perhaps in my lifetime we will see a better Russia.

> To recap, legislation passed through Russia's lower house in July, established two 'special administrative regions' within Russia - on Russky Island in the Sea of Japan and on Oktyabrsky, an island on a river in the Russian exclave of Kaliningrad.

---

[2]The Ministry for the Development of the Russian Far East, June 8, 2018.

[3]Russian Federation, Adopted by the state Duma on July 26, 2018, Approved by the Federation Council on 28 July 2018.

Looking forward, I believe the Middle East, Russia, and Central Asia have great promise ahead. China's Belt and Road Initiative is linking parts of Central Asia to the beginnings of the Western world and the long-distance train travel may open up cultural awareness from cross-continent adventure, apart from the billions in trade it will connect.

Case Study: The Aga Khan

> The voices of civil society will reflect and express the growing complexity of society, not as autonomous fragments, but as diversified institutions seeking the common good. And I believe that the voices of civil society can be among the most powerful forces in our time.—His Highness The Aga Khan, Brown University March 10, 2014

Prince Shah Karim Al Hussaini, the 49th Aga Khan is a hereditary Muslim imamate and a hereditary prince from the days of the Fatimid Caliphate.

In addition to his familial hereditary lineage, perhaps the most important aspect of Aga Khan's life is his foundation network. His foundation, the Aga Khan Development Network (AKDN) employs over 80,000 people and is a mixup of public charities, private foundations, for-profit endeavors, and charitable efforts. The AKDN has been building institutions and delivering essential services by creating schools and hospitals, newspapers and electricity generation plants, and social programs of all kinds. These services have helped improve the lives of millions of people in places as often forgotten by the Western world (Cairo, Kabul, Delhi, and Bamako).

Additionally, the Aga Khan receives tithes, annual donations from his loyal adherents. His adherents, the Ismailis Muslim community are spread across the world, from Karachi to Toronto.

> The AKDN is a group of private, international, non-denominational agencies working to improve living conditions and opportunities for people in specific regions of the developing world. The Network's organisations have individual mandates that range from the fields of health and education to architecture, rural development and the promotion of private-sector enterprise. Together, they work towards a common goal – to build institutions and programmes that can respond to the challenges of social, economic and cultural change on an ongoing basis. The AKDN works in close partnership with public and private institutions, including amongst others, governments, international organisations, companies, foundations, and universities. AKDN's social development agencies include the Aga Khan Health Services, Aga Khan Education Services,

Aga Khan Academies, the Aga Khan Agency for Microfinance, the Aga Khan Foundation, Aga Khan Agency for Habitat as well as two universities, the Aga Khan University and the University of Central Asia. The Aga Khan Trust for Culture coordinates AKDN's cultural activities, including the Aga Khan Award for Architecture, Historic Cities Programme, Aga Khan Music Initiative, Aga Khan Museum, and Aga Khan Program for Islamic Architecture (at Harvard and MIT). The Ismaili Muslims are a global, multi-ethnic community whose members, comprising a wide diversity of cultures, languages and nationalities, live in Central Asia, the Middle East, South Asia, Sub-Saharan Africa, Europe and North America.[4]

A Look at Africa

Africa has a mixed reputation on the international stage but in reality, there is plenty of affluence, from north to south, east to west. It is worth noting the two island nations of Mauritius and the Seychelles are world class in finance for the region. A recent misery index released by Barcelona-based Focus Economics S.A.R. listed Zimbabwe (#2), Nigeria (#6), and South Africa (#7) in the top ten of their "most miserable economies" which only complicates further analysis as Nigeria and South Africa are among the wealthiest countries in Africa. The most independent states are Nigeria, Botswana, Namibia, the island of Mauritius, the Seychelles, and South Africa (Figs. 10.1 and 10.2).

Nigeria is the leader in flat-out GDP spending and the economy has been soaring from oil prices and newfound wealth. Corruption abounds, but there has been an explosion of wealth that has made its way from Nigeria to the capitals of the world. With one of Africa's largest populations, Nigeria's success has cut both ways: high unemployment followed by a high number of unemployed youth has lead to uprisings which have sidelined Nigeria's growth, created regional wars and internal battles which have displaced millions. The terrorist group Boko Haram is to blame for much of the turmoil by taking advantage of the rural country in Nigeria where inequality is hitting the hardest and causing further instability with radicalization. Despite this, Nigeria has one of the highest weekly church attendance in the world, hovering around 70–80%. This pattern is unique among Africa, particularly Sub-Sahara, where most countries' populations consider religion highly important.[5]

[4]The Official Biography of His Highness the Aga Khan, www.akdn.org.
[5]Pew Research Center.

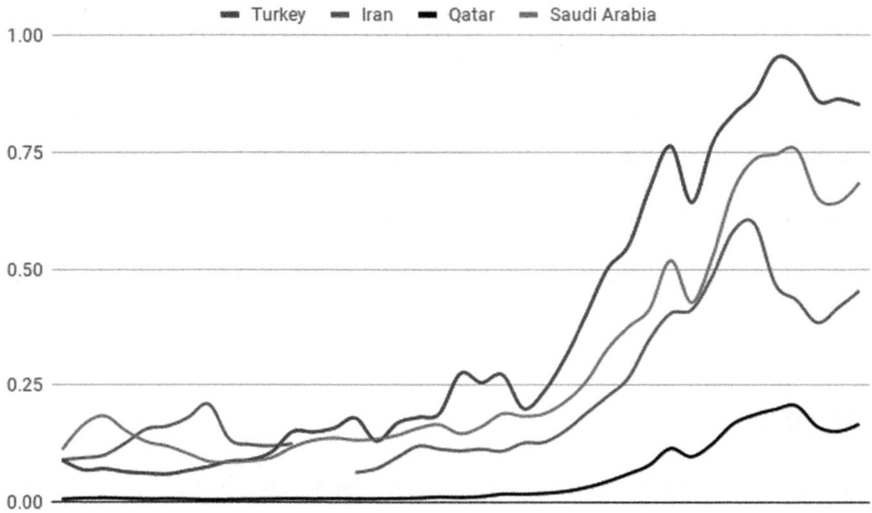

Fig. 10.1 Africa GDP Per Capita Compared

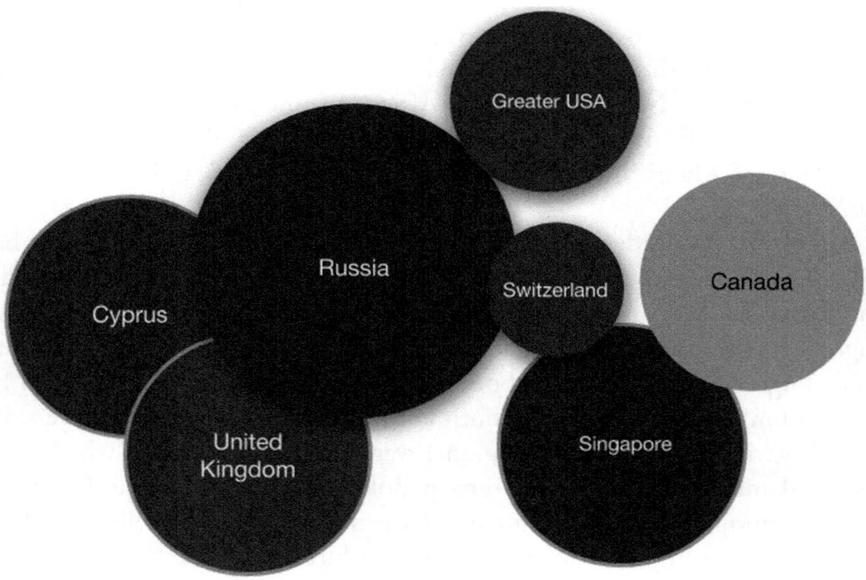

Fig. 10.2 Where Are New Family Offices Forming?

South Africa is widely developed with numerous industries and the continent's largest international trade activity and a lot of political volatility. This extends into other South African industries and sectors, including a venture capital scene and a culture for innovation. South Africa is the most developed country in Sub-Saharan Africa. Cape Town is a large metropolis with an incredible lifestyle but the political and economic instability detracts your average international investors, outside the very wealthiest and outside the inherited owners of industry. It makes for awful instability and low confidence levels.

Stonehage has two offices in South Africa, Cape Town, and Johannesburg. Their Cape Town location is near EY, the big four accountancy. The JSE (Johannesburg Stock Exchange Limited) is the 18th largest in the world with a total market capitalization of over one trillion dollars and the largest banks are First Rand; Standard Chartered; Nedbank, and ABSA. Most the wealth is dominated in Johannesburg, but wealth and power are Pretoria, Durban, and Cape Town, the latter in which has robust financial services. KwaZulu-Natal, is right after Johannesburg and third is the Western Cape.

Both hold established markets just behind Johannesburg, with significant enterprise and industry apart from the well-known exports from the Port of Durban to the agriculture and winery holdings in the neighborhoods and suburbs of Cape Town.

Not counting South Africa, wealth in Africa is concentrated in Lagos, Nigeria; Cairo, Egypt; Nairobi, Kenya; Luanda, Angola; Casablanca, Morocco; Accra, Ghana; Abidjan, Côte d'Ivoire and Addis Abada, Ethiopia. Surprisingly, the former bustling metropolis of Alexandria, Egypt is little more than a popular suburb of Cairo today. Luanda, Angola received some press a few years back as it was considered the most expensive city to rent an apartment in, largely due to oil concessions and expats in the oil industry with money to spend. Angola was embroiled in a terrible civil war that lasted from 1975–2002, so the robust growth is coming from a sustained period of autocratic control.

To take a closer look at advisors and specialists in the Africa market, Andersen Tax, the global consultancy has an extended presence in Africa. Counting their official offices in Lagos and Abuja, Nigeria and Nairobi, Kenya, the extended network has a footprint that covers most of Africa including Morocco, Senegal, Sierra Leone, Ivory Coast, Ghana, Niger, Nigeria, Cameroon, Angola, Namibia, Botswana, South Africa, Zimbabwe, Mozambique, Madagascar, Uganda, and Egypt. PwC, another consultancy, has the largest professional services footprint in the world employees over 9,000 people in 34 countries as of 2019 (Fig. 10.3).

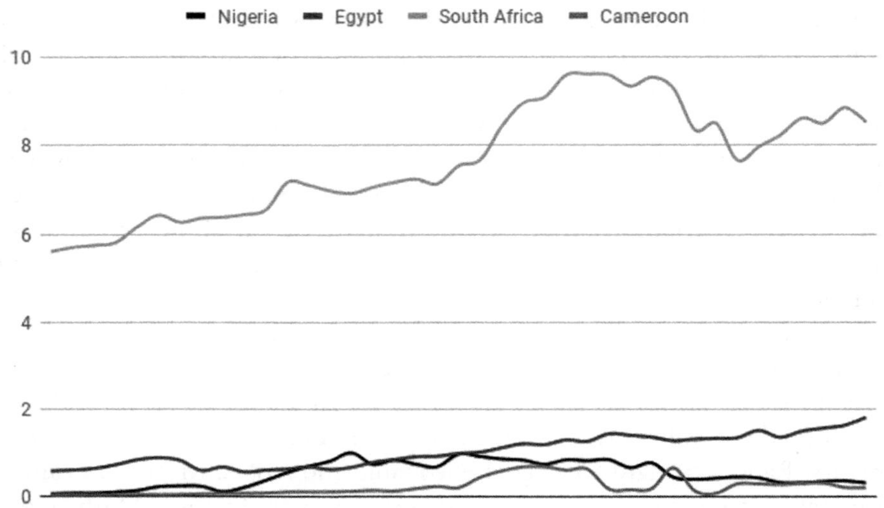

Fig. 10.3 Lack of Development or Competition?

Africa is not without its promises. Direct investment from China in African companies and resources has been a sizable catalyst for growth, and Sub-Saharan has counted on the China effect. It is rumored that an estimated 1 M Chinese have moved and settled in Africa over the past few decades. Much like European aristocrats leaving the old world for the new world to seek their fortune, the wave of Chinese immigrating to Africa is staggering and designed to develop and change the region. Investment has been pouring into build railways and oil refineries and to hope to instill peace in a fractured continent. Most of the investment has been devoted to infrastructure, from transport to energy to utilities, but real estate and technology have also been at the forefront. In a sport of modern quasi-colonization, China has been the catalyst to most of Africa's recent development in Sub-Sahara Africa. However, recent slowdowns in China have hit Africa particular hard, stifling growth and creating some uncertainty:

> China's economic ties with the region have deepened markedly over the past 20 years both through trade and financial linkages. China is the region's largest trading partner, accounting for about 20 percent of total trade. About 70 percent of the region's exports to China are related to commodities, particularly oil, minerals, and metals. About 20 percent of the region's imports are from China, and they are dominated by consumer goods imports (45 percent) and to a smaller extent physical capital goods and intermediates. Imports from China amounted to US$67.5 billion in 2017, compared with US$13.7 billion imports from the United States and US$79.7 billion imports from Europe. At

> the same time, China has become a major creditor for the region, providing significant lending to several countries as well as foreign direct investment (about 5 percent of total foreign direct investment). China's direct investment into the region is typically in metals and energy and flows primarily to resource-intensive countries. These investments are then channeled back into China through exports of metals and minerals. Stronger-than-anticipated tightening of global financial conditions could arise from a range of triggers besides escalating trade tensions, including higher-than-expected inflation in the United States, a "no-deal Brexit" withdrawal of the United Kingdom from the European Union, or a deeper-than-envisaged slowdown in China. Tighter global financial conditions could constrain financing and growth for many sub-Saharan African countries, especially the region's frontier economies, which have relied heavily on global markets to finance development needs.[6]

Despite China's pushback at the colonization label, it is very clear that China is a major player in Africa, if not modern Africa's most dominant investment partner to date. China is building railroads much like the British did. In 2015, Addis Ababa Light Rail opened; it was the first rapid transit in Sub-Saharan Africa, and the majority of financing came from China.

Structure and Planning: Mauritius and the Seychelles

The island of Mauritius was established as a financial hub in 1980. It was a deliberate government decision and came to aid divestment from Apartheid-riddled South Africa in the 1980–1990s. Geneva is a major hub for African services and family offices from Nigeria and South Africa. London is equally as popular and holds very close ties to Johannesburg and Cape Town, South Africa, despite the history of banking in South Africa and the establishment of the Seychelles and Mauritius as an offshore financial center. Investec, HSBC, Barclays, Standard Chartered, and Bank International Indonesia all have locations in Mauritius.

Mauritius is an island; the Seychelles is a grouping of islands or an archipelago. Both the nations have one thing in common and that is notable economic development and sustained stability. The Seychelles is one of the world's most developed tax havens and it is Africa's only high-income economy. The capital and largest city is Victoria, on the island of Mahe. In

[6]IMF, Sub-Saharan Africa Regional Economic Outlook: Recovery Amid Elevated Uncertainty April 2019.

recent years, the Central Bank of Seychelles has moved from a fixed position to that of a floating position. This reflects the nation's promise to efficiency and modernity, with an eye toward avoidance of the usual island nation problems of unemployment, substance abused and poverty, complete dependent on tourism. The Seychelles robust economic platform has allowed for a steady increase of domestic employment in the industrial sectors:

> Independent since 1976, the Seychelles is a relatively young democracy: the first multiparty presidential election was held in 1993 after the adoption of a new constitution. Seychelles' recent economic performance has been strong, benefiting from the continued growth of the tourism sector. Gross domestic product (GDP) growth in 2018 was 3.6%. Visitor numbers in 2018 were 361,844 (more than 3.5 times the resident population), a 3% increase over 2017. European markets remain key to the Seychelles tourism industry, but the sector is also benefiting from increases in tourists from other regions, facilitated in part by more airline connections. The formal unemployment rate was 3.5% in the third quarter of 2018, indicating a tight labor market consistent with robust recent economic conditions. Unemployment rates were higher for men (4.2%) than for women (2.9%). Youth unemployment was 14.5%.[7]

What the Seychelles lacks in family offices is more than made up for in the form of private foundations. Attracting businesses from all over the world, a private foundation in the Seychelles is an attractive vehicle for Indian, African, or European families with ties to Africa; Indian families may utilize the offshore zone and proximity to India for planning purposes.

Formed in the 1830s, Mauritius Commercial Bank is the oldest bank on the island. It is unique in its design as it is a bank with branches and ATMs, but also issues the local currency. Mauritius established the Mauritius Offshore Business Activities Act 1992. The purposes of such were to establish legal framework which governed the licensing of corporations, PWC and Deloitte both have offices here. Banks are well represented, including HCBS, Deutsche Bank, Bank of Baroda, and so are offshore management companies—created by the act to provide administration, trust registration, and trustee services.

[7]The World Bank In Seychelles.

What Is Next?

Broadly speaking, the Sahel and tropical Africa hold the next opportunities in Africa, both geographic regions are experiencing change at the moment. Political and economic change ahead, if successful policy and sustainability methods ratify and take hold, abundant resources, natural and human resources alike. The Sahel alone has a large youth population; over 64% are below 25 years of age[8] and part from youth leaving for larger cities for the burgeoning opportunity in Lagos, Nigeria and Abidjan, Ivory Coast.

SRI: Socially Responsible Investing

For decades I reckoned finance and economics to be the natural fundamentals of life, and to some degree a natural force. Now, I am able to see economics may be central to the economic-driven state systems we live in, but these economic systems have been evolved into monstrous systems manipulated by bad actors. These are far from natural orders.

The natural world and the cosmos have a system of order and sustainability; a system of disorder and destruction and an infinite timeline. In nature, we can see the prospects of the best design and efficient uses of materials and nature rarely uses more than it needs to. That has hardly been the case with the American world and the ungoverned capitalistic system. The reason I am devoting a chapter to Impact Investing & ESG is because it is without a doubt a permanent addition to finance, investment, and enterprise. Finance and banking have always wished to back the successes of tomorrow, willing to support old stalwarts if healthy enough and without headline risk.

Fortunately enough ESG and the ethos surrounding it became a sticking point and over time the ethos and ideas which came out of socially responsible investing (SRI) began to take a stronghold. I believe many of these frameworks came out of Buddhist Economics, Thailand's Sustainability Economy. The latter came out of a semi-religious oriented view on citizens, the state, and investments. Much like Sharia or Islamic financial, much like Kosher or Halal meat laws. Islamic financial laws were the main guide to stay away from liquor stores, gambling, and interest. Then came the 60 s and E. F. Schumacher's "*Small Is Beautiful: A Study of Economics As If People Mattered.*" This book was very influential and still is to this day, spawning numerous supporting groups and initiates like BerkShares.

[8]United Nations Africa Renewal (Information partner program within the UN's OSAA, AUDA-NEPAD and ECA commission).

Impact & ESG Investing in the Modern Age; Double Bottom Line (DBL) & Triple Bottom Line (TPL) & Social Return on Investment (SROI)

All of these associations' elements have uniformly different philosophies in their foundations but all agree on the need for enhanced ethical behavior in business and commerce. In developed countries all over organized religion is degrading. In the last few years, we have seen middle class in America gravitate to neo-conservatism and polarized charismatic leaders, a retaliation against the fears of progress and the years of globalization that did nothing in their eyes but help elites. While I will not go into great details in this publication, the mixture of the internet and globalization, as mentioned, flatten numerous obstacles, which in turn have developed in a compounded manner, rendering countless normal useless. Apart from that since 2015, it has become incredibly apparent that the United States has many changes ahead.

One well known group, the Rockefeller heirs (the 4th generation, after the five brothers) were pioneers in the field of SRI, ESG, and Impact and soon other American moneyed families followed suite, thus establishing the foundations of this industry segment. The viability has been proven, if only for a sample of successful responses. It is especially relevant to the FOs world as Impact Investing & ESG has been baked into the financial system and accepted en masse. Banks and financial institutions have already scaled back lending for carbon-heavy polluters and banks and financial institutions were the first to lead the developing emissions trading market.

Broadly speaking, Impact Investing is investing with the intention of creating change. Investing a social or a humanitarian or environmental purpose. It is no different than a beneficial cooperative or a beneficial corporation other than it often deals with developments and developing countries. ESG stands for Environmental, Sustainability, & Governance. A very important tool for the next century, ESG quantifies and qualifies around the three principles of ESG. To give an example, a private business decides to embody ESG principles by recycling trash and promoting a green way of life (E); The executives agree on a sustainability ethos and with involvement from the rest of the employee base, agree on the best ways to sustain business and operate on (S); the business decides that the executive management should receive a salary within reason of the lowest-paid employee on staff, in a bid to bring together the team by lessening inequality and to perhaps bring common sense to the forefront (G).

Double Bottom Line & Triple Bottom Line means adding an extra bottom line to your bottom line. Adjusting the profit and loss (P&L) to allow for additional features, you add a social bottom line and then perhaps an ESG bottom line. The social bottom line would denote community and the ESG bottom line would denote adherence to ESG principles. In essence, you take out straight profits and share the wealth, instead of buying a $100,000.00 automobile to avoid writing corporate taxes, instead, you chose to donate that money to a charity, or top off your employee's annual 401 k contributions. This is not a socialist form of thought—this is rooted in everyday life. Employees and especially entrepreneurs spend a major portion of their lives strapped to work and career, that unsustainability only increases with affluence and wealth. At the end of the day, we are all humans and we all have basic needs.

SRI or SROI is achieved by applying standard IRR and ROI investment principles to social and community-focused endeavors. While it differs from a beneficial corporation, it is similar in nature. As the CGIAR Research Program on Climate Change, Agriculture and Food Security (CCAFS) states:

> the SROI methodology has evolved over the last decade through several iterations. A term originating from Return on Investment (ROI) used by traditional investors for valuing purely financial returns, SROI is a framework for measuring and accounting for a broader concept of value by incorporating social, environmental and economic costs and benefits. SROI is about value, rather than money alone. The SROI process involves reviewing the inputs, outputs, outcomes and impacts made and experienced by stakeholders. Using a visual 'Impact Map', SROI tells the story of how change is being created by measuring and putting a monetary value on social, environmental and economic outcomes. While traded goods are valued using the prevailing market price, estimating the positive (or negative) social value of non-traded, non-market goods that are common in the environment is a more reflective process. SROI thus requires the use of financial proxies to achieve these quantifications.[9]

In the Book "*Let Me People Go Surfing*" Patagonia founder Yvon Chouinard shares his outlook on business, philosophy, and life. While Patagonia is a world-renowned company worth billions that was never the entire reason for forming the company. Nor was profit making the companies only concern. At Patagonia's headquarters in Ventura, California if the surf break is good you can break for surfing. While this may raise an eyebrow to some, it is perfectly reasonable so long as employees are performing. Silicon Valley does the same thing by offering perks that help with all sorts of daily life events

[9]Community-based Adaptation Costing: Working Paper No. 16. CGIAR Research Program on Climate Change, Agriculture and Food Security (CCAFS).

like childcare; free food; bring your pet to work, and working remote. While Chouinard may be following the prototypical California dream with surf time instead of Google's food hall, he is ahead of the game. Last century, we departed from local foods and local businesses and sat back as cities were destroyed from white flight and bedroom communities came to rule America. Year over year, growth may work for some corporations and hedge funds but for everyone else, it is no longer a reality. Add to this the realities from COVID-19 and slow food, slow capital and a slower way of life in America is no longer on the fringe.

Local business, local life, and now local currency. Historically, local municipalities and even banks printed their own banknotes. This practice has long stopped, but there are a number of complementary currencies floating about and they are not crypto-coins like Bitcoin. Bitcoin fulfilled a need for secondary currency in the global marketplace, and many have been enthusiastic about its development, but if we look to the past we can see that the future is very much rooted in local minded operations, when it comes to secondary currencies. This might mean eating local, shopping local, or just paying attention to the localities around you. BerkShares and their BerkShares Dollars are such examples. Headquartered in Great Barrington, Massachusetts, BerkShares has been a success, if not only for the movement but also the sponsorship and continuing support:

> BerkShares, Inc. is the place-based, democratically structured non-profit organization that issues BerkShares, a local currency for the Berkshire Region. BerkShares, Inc. works in collaboration with participating local banks, local businesses, and local non-profit organizations to strengthen the Berkshire regional economy through a local currency program and related pursuits. The members of BerkShares, Inc. envision a diverse and resilient regional economy that supports and prioritizes responsible production and consumption, wherein community members rely on the land and each other to fulfill the basic needs of food, culture, clothing, shelter, and energy. Anyone in the Berkshire Region may spend BerkShares or accept BerkShares for payment. BerkShares can be obtained at participating bank branches in exchange for U.S. dollars at a rate of 95 cents per BerkShare. These federal dollars remain on deposit at the BerkShares Exchange Banks in order to allow citizens to redeem BerkShares for dollars at the same exchange rate. For example, 95 dollars yield 100 BerkShares and 100 BerkShares yield 95 dollars. BerkShares can be spent at face value to pay for the goods or services offered by participating businesses—for example, 10 BerkShares can be used for a $10 purchase.[10]

[10]BerkShares, Inc. http://www.berkshares.org/.

Buddhist Economics

If you read about the early days of capitalism, you quickly come to the conclusion that capitalism in its current unbridled form needs retooling. The early fur trading days of Astor produced a fabulous fortune but with little regard for humane treatment of animals, let alone giving any thought to gender equality or pensions. Buddhist Economics perhaps holds the monopoly on mindfulness, however, it is important to note that this school of thought came into the mass market in the 1970s, around the same time Rodale was busy putting together regenerative and organic agriculture. The elder Rodale had laid forth his groundbreaking work on organics in the 1940s, with the idea taking a while to establish serious footing.

Buddhist economics was kicked off when economist E.F. Schumacher became an advisor to the prime minister. His resulting work was a landmark and shaped an entire generation to think small and local:

> The Buddhist point of view takes the function of work to be at least threefold: to give a man a chance to utilize and develop his faculties; to enable him to overcome his ego-centeredness by joining with other people in a common task; and to bring forth the goods and services needed for a becoming existence. It is clear, therefore, that Buddhist economics must be very different from the economics of modern materialism, since the Buddhist sees the essence of civilisation not in a multiplication of wants but in the purification of human character. From a Buddhist point of view, this is standing the truth on its head by considering goods as more important than people and consumption as more important than creative activity.[11]

The country Bhutan has adapted GNU, which stands for Gross National Happiness. This is their benchmark for state and citizen wellbeing.

I have included an edited and abbreviated list of Bhutan's Nine Domains of Gross National Happiness. They are as follows:

(1) Psychological well-being
(2) Health
(3) Time use: Promoting a balance of efficient time use; promoting healthy time usage and personal use of time
(4) Education: Besides incorporating formal and informal education, the domain also tries to assess different types of knowledge, values, and skills, which are mostly acquired informally.

---

[11] E. F. Schumacher, "*Small Is Beautiful: A Study of Economics As If People Mattered.*"

(5) Cultural diversity and resilience: The culture domain looks at the diversity and strength of cultural traditions including festivals, norms, and the creative arts.
(6) Community vitality, promoting interaction and dialogue within communities.
(7) Good Governance
(8) Ecological diversity and resilience: Basically assess eco-friendly behavior patterns.
(9) Worthwhile living standards, financial security, and ownership. All vitally important for mental security.

A basis of BE is when all of your fundamentals are taken care of you can flourish as a person, but these should be common, global goals.

> The Sustainable Development Goals (SDGs), otherwise known as the Global Goals, are a universal call to action to end poverty, protect the planet and ensure that all people enjoy peace and prosperity. These 17 Goals build on the successes of the Millennium Development Goals, while including new areas such as climate change, economic inequality, innovation, sustainable consumption, peace and justice, among other priorities. The goals are interconnected – often the key to success on one will involve tackling issues more commonly associated with another.[12]

The 17 Sustainable Development Goals (SDGs) (Abbreviated & Edited)

Goal 1: End poverty & Hunger in its all forms everywhere
Goal 2: Find food security, better nutrition and promote regenerative and sustainable agriculture
Goal 3: Ensure healthy lives, promote well-being for everyone
Goal 4: Ensure inclusive and equitable quality education and promote lifelong learning to all
Goal 5: Ensure gender equality and empower all women and girls
Goal 6: Ensure availability and sustainable management of water and sanitation for all
Goal 7. Ensure access to affordable, reliable, sustainable, and modern energy for all

[12]United Nations, Sustainable Development Goals.

Goal 8: Promote Sustainable Economic Growth, Full and Productive Employment, and Decent Work for All
Goal 9: Build resilient infrastructure, promote inclusive and sustainable industrialization, and foster innovation
Goal 10: Reduce inequality within and among countries
Goal 11: Make cities and human settlements safe and sustainable
Goal 12: Promote and establish sustainable consumption and production patterns
Goal 13: Combat Climate Change
Goal 14: Conserve and sustainably use the oceans, seas, and marine resources for sustainable development
Goal 15: Protect, restore, and promote sustainable use of terrestrial ecosystems, sustainably manage forests, combat desertification, and halt and reverse land degradation and halt biodiversity loss.
Goal 16: Promote peaceful and inclusive societies for sustainable development, provide access to justice for all and build effective, accountable and inclusive institutions at all levels
Goal 17: Strengthen the means of implementation and revitalize the Global Partnership for Sustainable Development.

Thailand's Sufficiency Economy (SE)

> The King of Thailand's philosophy of sufficiency economy highlights a balanced way of living. Three principles—moderation, reasonableness, and self-immunity—along with the conditions of morality and knowledge can be applied to any level of the society—from an individual to a country. This article proposes that the philosophy of sufficiency economy conveys new theory in addressing current development challenges, which are issues of institutions, human capital, environmental sustainability and the role of government. The philosophy of sufficiency economy, as a new paradigm of development, aims at improving human well-being as a development goal.

In Buddhism, you have ancient texts which guide monarchies and inherited seats as well as other elements; a Buddhist king must fill certain roles with certain attributes. While the investment and capitalistic world look to come full circle, there is sufficient evidence of state support in Buddhist areas.

As soon as this makes the transition into graduate economics and college-level economic development course, BE has a huge shot and laying a stronger foundation:

> Buddhist Economics (BE) could be a form of economics that presents an alternative to both neo-liberal economic policy and to Standard Textbook Economics (STE). However, it is by no means unambiguous what BE actually is, including among those dealing with it on a professional basis. Many if not most of the experts actually argue that methodologically, BE is not opposed to, but rather can be integrated into, STE, and that BE is what can be extrapolated from the teachings of the Buddha regarding economic policy. In Buddhism, as in almost all of the large religions, there is skepticism against earthly possessions and material success as goals per se. Nonetheless, contrary to Western popular assumptions, Buddhism is, and thus according to most experts also BE, not about asceticism but about the avoidance of suffering; the "middle path", while not a compromise but rather "getting things exactly right", looks from an outside perspective like one between two extremes, and thus wealth as such, or at least property, is not bad[13]

In late 2018, Professor Dietrich Christian Lammerts published *Buddhist Law in Burma: A History of Dhammasattha Texts and Jurisprudence, 1250–1850.* In this publication, Lammerts brings to light the corpus of Buddhist law that exists in Southeast Asia, particularly in Burma. The Dhammasattha is a codified legal system. The same in theory exists in Thailand with the SE mandate, and in Bhutan with GNU, despite those two examples not being codified systems. Burma, Bhutan, Thailand, and the Yogyakarta region of Indonesia are states that have written laws, constitutions, theories, and ethics supporting some element of universal happiness and support for all living peoples and creatures. As we separate BE from religion and incorporate more BE elements into law and finance it seems possible this framework could make its way into ESG and sustainable oriented investing and finance. As we have seen with climate finance and triple bottom line accounting, finance is a vehicle, which can rapidly influence normal operations. Much of the coal industry in the United States has been shut out of traditional financing due to pressures from environmental groups. If mindful groups continue to pressure corporate America and big corporations worldwide to make a worthwhile change, maybe it will happen.

I mentioned Rodale earlier, Jerome Irving Rodale (1898–1971) was an influential pioneer in organics and sustainability. He founded Rodale Organic Gardening Experimental Farm realizing farming needed to change. Rodale's method of Regenerative Agriculture is part of a next level organic and sustainability approach to farming and agriculture, but it has taken decades and decades of advocacy for such a method to take. When a consumer hears in

[13]The Reality and Diversity of Buddhist Economics, Working Papers in Technology Governance and Economic Dynamics, no. 69, 2016 Wolfgang Drechsler.

the media that meat is bad for the planet it is clear that the listener is hearing only a portion of the whole story. The same goes for the special report on a startup making meat in a test tube. None of this makes sense at first glance, and when you realize that the reason the arguments are being presented forth is from activism trying to balance out a century of industrial waste, the wires often get crossed. The truth is the global food supply is really messed up and over the past fifty years, we have become more separated from nature and our food and water sources than ever before. Apart from literal manpower, agriculture is very likely the first form of human manufacturing. Humans manipulated the environs to produce food, and over time figured out irrigation techniques and those led to moving water around and planting rice in water beds, etc. Then we moved onto protein and took over the forests, fields, and waterways. From vegetarian and vegan diets to whole food availability, greengrocery, and natural foods there is a lot of work to be done. This will only increase the need for investment in innovation and technology, in conjunction with changing tastes and food trends.

Key Principles of Islamic Finance (Sharia Finance)

Islamic Finance is a growing aspect of finance, which encompasses most of the Middle East and some of Central Asia. While different from ESG and Impact Investing, minus the religious aspects they have many commonalities. The basis is to stay away from haram. Haram means sin. Any money derived off of money is considered a sin. Companies dealing in tobacco and spirits are unworthy of investment and so is adult entertainment. All of the main vices are unworthy of any investment. Instruments fall into three categories: PLS, non-PLS, and fee-based. Islamic Finance is a growing segment that all financiers will have to adapt and learn—if not grow accustomed to the characteristics— over the next decade.

I have included an excerpt from the IMF which covers the basics of Islamic Finance:

> Islamic Finance Framework[14]:
> "Islamic finance is quite complicated, but the truth of the matter is there is a deep framework for loans and interest in Judaism, and most Abrahamic religions discuss the principle of debt and living debt free. The key principles of Islamic finance

[14]IMF Islamic Finance.

derive from principles in the Shariah legal code. Shariah jurisprudence does not distinguish between religious and other aspects of life, including transactions falling under either the political, economic, or social sphere (muamalat)."

Three Principles Govern Islamic Finance

Principle of equity: Made up of predetermined payments called "riba"—the principle of equity and wealth distribution is also the basis of a 2.5 percent levy on cash or in-kind wealth (zakat), imposed by Shari'ah on all Muslims who meet specific minimum levels of income and wealth to assist the less fortunate and foster social solidarity.

Principle of participation: Although commonly known as interest-free financing, the prohibition of riba does not imply that capital is not to be rewarded. According to a key Shari'ah ruling that "reward (that is, profit) comes with risk taking," investment return has to be earned in tandem with risk-taking and not with the mere passage of time, which is also the basis of prohibiting riba. Thus, return on capital is legitimized by risk-taking and determined ex post based on asset performance or project productivity, thereby ensuring a link between financing activities and real activities. The principle of participation lies at the heart of Islamic finance, ensuring that increases in wealth accrue from productive activities.

Principle of ownership: The rulings of "do not sell what you do not own" (for example, short-selling) and "you cannot be dispossessed of a property except on the basis of right" mandate asset ownership before transacting. Islamic finance has, thus, come to be known as asset-based financing, forging a robust link between finance and the real economy. It also requires preservation and respect for property rights, as well as upholding contractual obligations by underscoring the sanctity of contracts.

PLS Financing

Think profit and loss share. There are two types of PLS financing: musharakah and mudârabah.

"Musharakah" is a profit-and-loss sharing partnership and the most authentic form of Islamic financing. It is a contract of joint partnership where two or more partners provide capital to finance a project or own real estate or movable assets, either on a permanent or diminishing basis. Losses are shared in proportion to capital contribution.

"Mudârabah" is a profit-sharing and loss-bearing contract where one party supplies funding (financier as principal) and the other provides effort and management expertise (entrepreneur) with a view to generating a profit.

Losses are shared. This mimics a GP-LP relationship otherwise known as a limited partnership.

Non-PLS Financing

Non-PLS contracts are most common in practice. They are generally used to finance consumer and corporate credit, as well as asset rental and manufacturing. Non-PLS financing instruments include murâbaḥah, ijārah, salam, and istisna'.

"Murâbaḥah" is a popular Shari'ah-compliant sale transaction mostly used in trade and asset financing. The bank purchases the goods and delivers them to the customer, deferring payment to a date agreed by the two parties. The expected return on murâbaḥah is usually aligned with interest payments on conventional loans, creating a similarity between murâbaḥah sales and asset-backed loans. However, murâbaḥah is a deferred payment sale transaction where the intention is to facilitate the acquisition of goods and not to exchange money for more money (or monetary equivalents) over a period of time. Unlike conventional loans, after the murâbaḥah contract is signed, the amount being financed cannot be increased in case of late payment or default, nor can a penalty be imposed, unless the buyer has deliberately refused to make a payment.

"Istisna'" is a contract in which a commodity can be transacted before it comes into existence. The unique feature of istisna' (or manufacturing) is that nothing is exchanged on the spot or at the time of contracting. It is perhaps the only forward contract where the obligations of both parties are in the future. In theory, the istisna' contract could be directly between the end user and the manufacturer, but it is typically a three-party contract, with the bank acting as intermediary.

"Salam" is a form of a forward agreement.

"Ijārah" is a contract of sale of the right to use an asset for a period of time. It is essentially a lease contract and since ownership remains with the leaser, the asset can be repossessed in case of nonpayment by the lessee. The leaser is also responsible for asset maintenance, unless damage to the leased asset results from lessee negligence. This element of risk is required for making ijārah payments permissible. This mimics a triple net lease (NNN).

Fee-Based

Islamic banks offer a wide spectrum of fee-based services using three types of contracts, wakalah, kafalah, or ju'ala. They are usually auxiliary to the main murâbaḥah and mudârabah transactions, though they generate various types of fees and commissions. The fee-based services provided by Islamic banks include bank transfers, issuing letters of credit and guarantees, credit cards, and offering collection and safe-custody services, mostly used in trade financing. Wakalah results from the bank acting as the agent of a customer in a trade transaction or issuing a letter of credit facility.

10,000 Women

Goldman Sachs is a leader in forward thinking and best practice planning; long perceived as a gigantic investment bank, in recent years Goldman has created Marcus, a no-fee personal loans & high-yield online savings platform, as well as spearheading initiatives like "10,000 Small Businesses" which is a small business focused program and the program "10,000 Women" which is geared much like the aforementioned program but for women entrepreneurs. In 2018, Goldman Sachs Group announced a plan to include women in their executive leadership, to strive for an equitable balance of genders employed with equal pay. Overrepresentation of males has long plagued Wall Street, as less than 25% of upper management in major financial firms are led by women. Goldman has been in the family office space for many years apart from just wealth management, utilizing their deep bench and experience to help family's source deals and figure out complex investments.

> Goldman Sachs offers a broad suite of resources for family office clients to meet their objectives across asset allocation, financing, and public and private market investing. We work with family offices whose AUM ranges from $100mm to $50bn+ AUM. We shaped our business to cater to recent trends within the family office space, including an expanded global presence and hedge fund to family office conversions. This client segment continues to increase its allocation to direct, private investments, given the meaningful opportunity set private markets have presented over the past 10 years. Shifts within the public markets include a focus on investing in high quality companies and using derivatives for arbitrage opportunities. Beyond markets, family offices place value on tax efficient investing, with an influx of recent inquiries around opportunity zones and hard assets. Perhaps the most important factor for family offices is access to customizable coverage across asset classes and geographies. This cohort tends to place significant importance on networking

with like-minded families to share top-of-mind ideas, themes, and best practices.[15]

Research from our research unit, HCG Insight, finds that when it comes to managing the household finances, American middle-class and upper-middle-class household spending is controlled by women. That means the women have the upper hand in financial management decisions in the household. To further my point, in American middle-class households, the female earner is often the highest income earning member of the household. When it comes to impoverished families the mother is almost always the chief provider. While these statements support female leadership in finance and economics, it happens much faster when global leaders and enterprising families make the push toward equitable equality.

Bibliography

See Ministry for Europe and Foreign Affairs, Joint statement by the E3 Foreign Ministers Jean-Yves Le Drian (France), Heiko Maas (Germany), Jeremy Hunt (United Kingdom).

See statement, The Ministry for the Development of the Russian Far East, June 8, 2018.

See Russian Federation, Adopted by the state Duma on July 26, 2018, Approved by the Federation Council on 28 July 2018.

See the Aga Khan, official biography at the Aga Khan Development Network.

See research of Sub-Sahara Africa from the Pew Research Center.

See IMF, Sub-Saharan Africa Regional Economic Outlook: Recovery Amid Elevated Uncertainty April 2019.

See Report, The World Bank In Seychelles.

See United Nations Africa Renewal (Information partner program within the UN's OSAA, AUDA-NEPAD and ECA commission).

Community-based Adaptation Costing: Working Paper No. 16. CGIAR Research program on Climate Change, Agriculture and Food Security (CCAFS).

See BerkShares, Inc. http://www.berkshares.org/.

E. F. Schumacher, "*Small Is Beautiful: A Study of Economics As If People Mattered*".

See United Nations, Sustainable Development Goals.

The Reality and Diversity of Buddhist Economics, Working Papers in Technology Governance and Economic Dynamics, no. 69, 2016 Wolfgang Drechsler.

See IMF Islamic Finance.

Sandy Bernhardt, Managing Director, Goldman Sachs Group, Inc., May 2019.

[15] Sandy Bernhardt, Managing Director, Goldman Sachs Group, Inc., May 2019.

11

Conclusion

In conclusion, family offices have a bright future. They are largely unregulated and generally closely held family interests; the structure of SFO, MFO or private office is useful for a variety of reasons from succession, to estate planning and financial oversight; and there is almost no reason to propose regulation, in fact there is ample evidence to support municipalities, states, and countries offering subsidiaries to attract family offices.

Perhaps the most important aspect of the future of the family office world is where wealth is created and in return where that wealth is invested, domiciled, and put to work. As we have seen in the Middle East, since the 1970s the public–private framework of oil rich nations has been developed to the point that many of the family offices in the Middle East are now global in nature. I think we will see more of this. The push back from intensive globalization and the ongoing COVID pandemic, which began in 2020, have forced politicians to focus on their home turf, making sure jobs, industry and small business survive. Globalization hasn't ended as a result of this, but it has been dialed back. Perhaps we will see an uptick in family offices investing internationally and going international for opportunities, but to be honest we are as likely to see FO's retreat and invest locally. While it is clear that while family offices have many similarities, every family office has unique attributes.

It is fair to assume that eventually the power hold of family offices and generational capital will shift from the English-speaking world to Asia, in the process becoming more inclusive and incorporating dramatic cultural shifts which will include new stakeholders from Asia, Africa, the Middle East, Russia, and India.

C. Hagan, *Global Family Office Investing*,
https://doi.org/10.1007/978-3-030-18224-3_11

Works cited

Ahmed, Azam, "Soros to Close His Fund to Outsiders". *New York Times*. September 26, 2011.

Cannadine, David, "Class in Britain." Penguin Books Limited, London, UK, 2000.

Schumacher, Ernst Friedrich, "Small Is Beautiful: A Study of Economics As If People Mattered." Harper & Row, London, UK, 1973.

Vogel, Ezra F., "The Four Little Dragons." Harvard University Press, Cambridge, Massachusetts, 1991.

Yasheng, Huang, "Capitalism with Chinese Characteristics: Entrepreneurship and the State." Cambridge University Press, New York, NY, 2008.

C. Hagan, *Global Family Office Investing*,
https://doi.org/10.1007/978-3-030-18224-3

Index

C. Hagan, *Global Family Office Investing*,
https://doi.org/10.1007/978-3-030-18224-3

GPSR Compliance

The European Union's (EU) General Product Safety Regulation (GPSR) is a set of rules that requires consumer products to be safe and our obligations to ensure this.

If you have any concerns about our products, you can contact us on ProductSafety@springernature.com

In case Publisher is established outside the EU, the EU authorized representative is:

Springer Nature Customer Service Center GmbH
Europaplatz 3
69115 Heidelberg, Germany

Batch number: 10732885

Printed by Printforce, the Netherlands